God's Great Creation

by

Bennie Morris Byrd

DORRANCE PUBLISHING CO., INC.
PITTSBURGH, PENNSYLVANIA 15222

ISBN # 0-8059-5374-4
Printed in the United States of America

First Printing

For information or to order additional books, please write:
Dorrance Publishing Co., Inc.
643 Smithfield Street
Pittsburgh, Pennsylvania 15222
U.S.A.
1-800-788-7654
Or visit our web site and on-line catalog at *www.dorrancepublishing.com*

Scripture was taken from:
The King James Bible (KJV)
The New Nave's Topical Bible (NIV)
Used by permission.

CONTENTS

ACKNOWLEDGMENT

Rev. and Mrs. Amos Landry
Rev. and Mrs. Eddie C. Jones
Arthur and Beverly Morris
James W. Morris, Sr.
Derek and April Marino
James W. Morris, Jr.
Charles and Isabell Barney
Alba and Elneda Mallory
Willie and Biona Miller
Ocie and Majorie Turner
Emory and Ivy Tungsvik
Robert and Joyce Oatis
Georgia M. Webster
Ola M. Harris
Luretha Reed
Arnada Jones

Mable Jackson
Florence Whelock
Tracena Bratton
Bettie Smith
Doris Jenkins
Betty Tolbert
Julia Lee
Audrey McNeil
Jewel Hall
Bettie Martin
Hattie L. Rice
Lorene Nelson
Toni Washington
Maryee Johnson
Josephine Lynch
Bertha Jinkins

My acknowledgment and gratitude to God (The Great Creator) for giving me the inspirations, wisdom, courage, and the patience to write the book of my dreams-disclosing the realness of God, His eternal love and mercy for all mankind.

PREFACE

Acknowledging God as the Creator of the human race-focusing on the conclusion of life from an Eternal viewpoint-through the sovereign operation within the Divine act of God-the giver-the ruler and maker of all that exists. Please note: Gen. 1:1-5 and John 1:1.

The Scriptures tell us: God foreknew us-loving us with an everlasting love before the world was created. God, with unsearchable Divine wisdom, looked upon us perceiving the future needs of all mankind. Please note: (Rom. 8:28-31, Eph. 1:4-7). God is the Rock. Indeed, His works are perfect and everlasting.

My desire is to provide a vivid picture of life. God is life, the only Source of life. I have steadfast hope, because the prophecies and the promises of God are Eternal. I am expressing my perception of the past and the present, as only God is aware of the secrets of the future; still, God purposed, making known to us the things that we are to know (Deut. 29:29). The displays of His Divine works are in abundance-they are, indeed, in perfect visual forms from the ends of the earth.

I trust there will be something noted in this book such as the Bible truths or maybe some facts and subjective ideas that will prove to be revealing and esteeming as an enhancing inspiration that might influence all mankind that God is real-purposely as a beacon of light for the younger generation, and generations to come, that they might also become aware of God's Divine existence and from this awareness, footsteps will be made for Christ early in life (Eccl. 12:1). Indeed, this is pleasing to God. Jesus said, "Suffer the little children to come unto Me, and forbid them not...for of such is the kingdom of God..."(Niv)

I believe that it is my reasonable service as a Christian to be Christ-like, proclaiming to others the love of God (John 3:16) that all might have the right to the Tree of Life. Eph. 2:10 tells us, "For we are His workmanship, created in Christ Jesus unto good works, which God hath before ordained that we should walk in them." It is also pleasing to God that all believers eagerly reach out to both the young and the old, that all might become aware of God's grace and be filled with the fullness of God. Man must make the choice and decision (Rom. 10:9-13).

The Bible claims to be the Inspired Word of God. The Bible tells us, "All Scripture is given by inspiration of God, and is profitable for doctrine, for reproof, for correction, for instruction in righteousness: The Divine wisdom of God can not be measured." God's plan and purpose for all mankind is written in His Holy Word. It is noted that the presentation of certain portions of the Old and the New testament have been purposely acknowledged, that we might acquire a vivid and better understanding of God's Holy Word. It is a fact, with fervent prayer, the Spirit will open both our eyes and minds as we study, exploring the Inspired Word of God. Thy word is a lamp unto my feet-and a light unto my path (Ps. 119:105). God's Word is a guiding Holy Light that leads the footsteps of all mankind into the path of God's righteousness, that all might learn of Him. Jer. 29:13 tells us, "And ye shall seek me, and find me, when ye shall search for me with all your heart."

The history of the Old Testament unfolds insight and the background of the record of all creation, revealing the knowledge of historical truths, noting the promises and the prophecies of God, that point to the New Testament. We note the types as the shadow of the things to come. Christ is indeed the theme (subject) of the Bible.

From the beginning, God made man (Gen. 2:7-8) for His Divine purpose and plan, according to His will. God was in the foreknowledge of the lives of all mankind (Rom. 5:12-21). Step by step, God purposed a redemptive plan for all mankind through Jesus Christ (Gal. 4:4-7).

We note the birth, the commission, and the authorship of Moses-He was God's agent for the deliverance of the children of Israel out of Egypt; the same God is delivering souls for His purpose and plan today. It is a fact-God's purpose and plan cannot be nullified. God's Word is Holy, an everlasting light that precedes the footsteps of His dear children. Rom. 13:12 tells us, "The night is far spent, the day is at hand: let us therefore cast off the works of the darkness, and let us put on the armor of light." There is no darkness in the Word of God-His Word leaves us without the shadow of doubts and excuses. "Should we neglect His priceless sacrifice?" I Cor. 5:7 tells us, "For even Christ our passover…is sacrificed for us…"

This question was asked by a concerned young adult, "Where was Jesus all the time before He was born?" The question was answered immediately-special Scriptures were quoted and given for future study to aid in promoting and preparing the mind for a better understanding of the Bible truths. There is no respect of person with God. Man must make the decision. Jesus said, "Follow me."

Let us ponder and recognize the things of the Spirit, always acknowledging God and His grace. In Him we have all things-love, peace, and joy unfolding from within, overflowing like a mighty river of life (John 7:38), refreshing as the morning dew, or the falling rain upon the thirsty land. "My doctrine shall drop as the rain-my speech…shall distill as the dew..."

INTRODUCTION

The Source of Life

Have you ever pondered or become seized with wonder, visioning the image of the origin of the human race? Wholly realizing and acknowledging the Creator as the Sovereign God who formed us from the dust of the ground? Please note: (Gen. 2:7-8). Indeed, God is life-the only Source of life. "For with thee is the fountain of life." (Ps. 36:9).

The steps that caused sin to enter into the world was man's disbelief and disobedience to God's command (Gen. 2:16-17). Because of one man's offense (Gen. 3:6), we were all made sinners (Rom. 5:12). Nevertheless, "God so loved the world...(John 3:16). We were loved with the everlasting love of God, before the world began (II Tim. 1:9). We have reasons to praise God with gratitude. However, first of all, let us praise and worship Him for who He is. God is Sovereign, His greatness is unsearchable (Rom. 11:33).

It is a fact that many footsteps are made, knowingly walking in the path of sin, preferring not to obey the laws of God which sometimes appear to be the willful lot of mankind. (Let us note: Gen. 3:1-13; Rom. 5:12-19; I Pet. 3:20).

In the Old Testament, the Scripture tells us that during the bondage of the children of Israel (Deut. 1:30-38), they were a rebellious generation-a nation of people that rebelled against God and their appointed leaders. They rejected the God who saved (delivered) them (I Sam. 10:18-19). It is a fact that disbelief and disobedience to God is sin. The Scripture (Is. 59:2-3) tells us, "Sin separates us from God, however, God's love for the human race is everlasting. I am the vine-ye are the branches: He that abideth in me-and I in him-the same bringeth forth much fruit: for without me ye can do nothing" (John 15:5).

This book is about love and life, the past and the present. Indeed, only God holds the secrets of the future. God is Eternal, God is love, and God is life. God always was and God always will be, in whose hand is the soul of every living thing and the breath of all mankind.

We were created in the image of God for His purpose. We were created for the glory of God (Is. 43:7) according to the Divine will of God. Let us keep this fact in mind: The Divine wisdom of God is unsearchable and cannot be measured. "Who hath put wisdom in the inward parts?...or who hath given understanding to the heart?" (Job 38:36-37).

The path of life is a journey. During the course of the pilgrimage it pleased God when we become partakers of His grace (Eph. 2:5-8). It is a fact that we are not to know when, nor where, our footsteps will end. However, it is wise to walk with a clean heart. Satan dwells in unclean temples.

Each individual has a life to live-none other can live it-nevertheless, fate can destroy it. Being unreceptive to spiritual doctrine or ideas is an individual choice and decision, nevertheless, our day in judgment is sure to come (Rom. 2:5; 14:10; Gen. 3:19). Jas. 4:14 says, "Where as ye know not what shall be on the morrow. For what is your life? It is even a vapor-that appeareth for a little time-and then vanisheth away." Maintaining a spiritual fellowship with God is indeed Christ-like. Without the blessings of His favors we would be nothing. It is because of God's love and mercy we are not consumed (Gal. 5:14-15).

God is the Rock. His ways and works are perfect, great, and marvelous. In the way of righteousness is life, and in the pathway thereof there is no death (Prov. 12:28). Let us remember, all sin is unrighteousness. Sin can mar, hindering our spiritual growth. Our sins are no secret before God (Jer. 16:17). Mercy and truth are met together, righteousness and peace have kissed each other (Ps. 85:10). The great sacrifice (John 3:16) for sin was grace. God's unlimited love and mercy was grace through faith in the blood of Christ Jesus (Rom. 3:24-26). This favor we did not deserve.

Divine guidance is an infallible promise given by God to all mankind (Ps. 32:8). It is wise to seek counsel early in life (Prov. 11:14), as life's success comes from divine blessings from above. Seek, and learn who God is. Age is not limited. Please note: (Eccl. 12:1) "Remember now thy Creator...in the days of thy youth..."

The time will come in life when we must separate from our families and friends. Each individual must take the time to concentrate, considering with future visions, as footsteps are being made towards higher goals. Indeed, success waits to become the desired conquest as the chosen paths of life are pursued, step-by-step.

Some individuals will turn to the left, some will be undecided, and some will turn to the right. Nevertheless, no matter when nor where the snaring obstacles may befall, there will always be a guiding light, even in the darkness of the nights. Indeed, we are never, never alone. God is always there for us, observing, whispering softly, "This is the way...walk ye in it..." (Is. 30:21). "Let no man despise thy youth...but be thou an example of the believers...." "Till I come, give attendance to reading-to exhortation-to doctrine" (I Tim. 4:12-13).

chapter 1

The Recognition of Life

Webster's Dictionary defines life as a living being-especially a human being-the time a person or thing is alive. Life is the recognition of a very precious gift. This individual gift (Gen. 2:7) is one of God's creations, predetermined through the sovereign act of God's election and His elect. It is a fact that God is in the foreknowledge of all things. The Scriptures tell us of God's eternal plan-purposed before the world began (Eph. 1:4-5; II Tim. 1:9). God's wisdom is unlimited and unsearchable.

God is the Creator, the Supreme Being having no beginning and no ending. God is life—the Source of life. God is the preserver and sustainer of life. God is love, His love is unbounded and incessant (Rom. 5:8-11). God was, God is, and God will always be the ruler of the universe. God is Holy—perfect in all righteousness (Ps. 111:3).

The Bible is the Inspired Word of God, revealing unto us the everlasting truths that we are to know (Deut. 29:29) about God and His Holy Word. God is the way, the truth, and the life. In whose hand is the soul of every living thing and the breath of all mankind (Job 12:10).

Before the actuality of creation (Gen. 1:1), the Word (John 1:1-5; 17:5) existed with God the Creator eternally. He is the immortal Supreme Being, having no beginning and no ending of life. "Was with God...and was God..." (John 1:1).

The Word was actively united with God in the work of creation (vs. 2-5), created by the Spirit-power at God's command (Heb. 11:3). The Word was Divinely represented as an active agent in the workmanship of creation, (Ps. 104:30-31) created by the Spirit according to the will of God. "The fellowship of the Divine mystery was made possible through the manifestation of the Spirit...within the sovereign act of God-according to God's election and His elect..." (Eph. 3:9). God is omnipotent (Eph. 3:11). At God's appointed time, by the power of His Spirit, the work of creation was done. Let us note: "For He spake-and it was done-He commanded-and it stood fast." (Ps. 33:9)

This Divine event will be related, "And the Word was made flesh,...and dwelt among us..." (John 1:14-15).

The Bible tells us that the angels are heavenly beings created by God. Ps. 148.1-5 says, "Praise ye the Lord...Praise ye the Lord from the heavens..." Praise ye Him, all His angels. Praise ye Him, all ye stars of light. "Praise Him...ye heavens of heavens..." Let them praise the name of the Lord for He commanded and they were created.

The Scriptures tell us the angels are holy, immortal, invisible, obedient, and countless in number. Indeed, God is the Supreme Ruler of the universe. God has revealed in His Word, the Holy Bible, "The secret things belong unto the Lord our God: But the things that we are to know-comprehend and obey...God has revealed them unto all mankind-from generation to generation..." (Deut. 29:29).

The Scriptures have revealed the prehistory of God's creation of heavenly beings. The Bible tells us that the angels are God's spiritual messengers-communicating solely for the purposes of God (Ps. 103:20-21; 104:4). The angels are servants, rendering and performing their special duties at God's command (Heb. 1:14; 12:22. Also please note Ex. 3:1-2; Ps. 34:7; Mat. 1:20-21; Luke 1:26-38; 2:10). The angels are God's perfect creations. "God is the Rock...His work is perfect...for all His ways are judgment..." (Deut. 32:4)

God has revealed in His word (Job 4:18; Jude 6;), unfolding the preexistency of iniquity (transgression) found in some angelic beings, noting the fate of their first estate (Jude 6). II Pet. 2:4 tells us, "For if God spared not the angels that sinned-but cast them down to hell-and delivered them into chains of darkness-to be reserved unto judgment; "God is Infinite." God is just...and true..."

The Bible tells us that an archangel is a chief angel. It is noted that Lucifer was ranked as one of the chief archangels (messengers), an angel of the highest order occupying the celestial hierarchy. "Lucifer was created perfect-yet, with all of his knowledge, brightness, and beauty...iniquity was found in thee..." (Ezek. 28:15) The prehistory of sin is noted (Is. 14:12-15): Lucifer rebelled against the God who governs him. "Lucifer willed within his heart...with the desire to ascend (with sovereignty) into heaven...equally in control-or above the King Eternal...the Most High...."

Indeed, God is in constant control, with uttermost surveillance of the entire universe. He never slumbers. It is a fact that no matter where or when, iniquity is the depth of sin, the transgression of God's law (Jude 6). Lucifer, (now known as Satan the deceiver-the devil), was cast out of heaven onto the earth, and all his angels with him. Please note: (Luke 10:18; Rev. 12:7-9).

At the creation of the earth (Gen. 1:1-2; John 1:1-2) the Bible tells us that the angels revealed their joy, "Who hath laid the measures thereof, if thou knowest? Or who hath stretched the line upon it? Whereupon are the foundations thereof fastened? Or who laid the cornerstone thereof; when the morning stars sang together, and all the sons of God shouted for joy?" (Job 38:5-7) "To whom then will ye liken me, or shall I be equal? saith the Holy One." (Is. 40:25) Again, God is omnipotent and everlasting.

The Bible tells us everything that God made was good.

First day:	light
Second day:	firmament
Third day:	seas, land, and vegetation
Fourth day:	heavenly bodies
Fifth day:	animal life of sea and air
Sixth day:	(1) animal life of earth
Sixth day:	(2) man

"And the Lord God formed man of the dust of the ground, and breathed into his nostrils the breath of life; and man became a living soul." And the Lord God took the man and put him into the garden of Eden to dress it and to keep it. And the Lord God commanded the man, saying, "Of every tree of the garden thou mayest freely eat: But of the tree of the knowledge of good and evil...thou shalt not eat of it..."

It is a fact that only God is in the foreknowledge of the future. The Lord God made a help meet for Adam. "And the rib which the Lord God had taken from the man...made he a woman...and brought her unto the man..." And they were both naked-the man and his wife-and were not ashamed. Please note: (Gen. 2:21-25).

A beast (Satan's craft) appeared unto the woman in the form of a serpent (II Cor. 11:14). I Tim. 2:14 tells us, "And Adam was not deceived-but the woman being deceived was in transgression. Eve took of the fruit thereof...and did eat-and gave also unto her husband with her-and he did eat...." Adam was aware, and understood God's command. He was not coaxed into eating the forbidden fruit-he yielded to the deceptive way of Satan instead of obeying the command of God. Adam willingly acted on his own. Adam sinned because of disbelief and disobedience to God's command. Here we note the fall of the first created man (Gen. 3:).

At this point, sin entered into the world-we were all made sinners. Ro. 5:12 tells us, "*Wherefore, as by one man sin entered into the world* and death by sin; and so death passed upon all men, for that all have sinned." Because of the sin of our first parent the whole world was made guilty before God, from the children of Adam, from generation to generation, even to the last birth on earth.

As a consequence of Adam's offense, sin entered into the world. The death sentence was passed (Rom. 5:12) upon the human race. God's redemptive plan was essential (I Peter 1 :18-20) for the remission of sins (Mat. 26:28; Rom. 3:23).

"O Lord...how manifold are thy works! In wisdom hast thou made them all..." (Ps. 104:24). Indeed, I believe all of God's works were, and are, purposed for Divine reasons. Prov. 20:18 tells us, "...Every purpose is established by counsel... For the Lord of hosts hath purposed-and who shall disannul it? And his hand is stretched out and who shall turn it back?" (Is. 14:27)

"The promise of the Redeemer is unfold." Genesis 3:15 tells us, "And I will put enmity between thee and the woman (Mat. 13:25, 28), and between thy seed and her seed; it shall bruise thy head (Rom. 16:20) and thou shalt bruise his heel (Rev. 12:7)." Throughout the Old Testament, we note that God was constantly unfolding His prophecies and promises. They are all, indeed, infallible and everlasting.

Both Adam and his wife Eve ate the forbidden fruit, merely represented as a symbol of rejection, noting the broken dedicated trust in God's way of holiness, the sacred trust in God's Divine plan. Nevertheless, who can hinder the works of the Almighty God? To this day, and from generation to generation, Satan the devil is constantly endeavoring to disannul the perfect, marvelous works of God. It is literally indicated (Is. 14:12-14; Ezek. 28:15-17) in the Word. Lucifer was beautiful and perfect in his ways. From the realization of this fact, pride entered his heart. The first sin in the realm of the history of eternity is noted, noting; (II Pet. 2:4-5, Jude v.6, Rev. 20:10).

Indeed, the judgment of God for all mankind stands unerring and inescapable. I John 5:17 tells us, "All unrighteousness is sin " Remember the former things of old for I am God, and there is none else; I am God, and there is none like me. "(I AM THAT I AM)."

Adam, our first parent, willingly (Gen. 2:16-17; 3:6) disobeyed God's command. The Scripture (Rom. 5:12-14) tells us, "By one man sin entered into the world." The fall (Gen. 3:1-24) of man is noted. Nonetheless, within the spiritual mind one can conceive the imparting of God's righteous ways, noting His love and mercy-the rendering as a divine refuge unto (sinners) those that were in a state of dire distress. The Scripture tells us, "And the eyes of them both were opened, and they knew that they were naked." Both Adam and the woman tried to cover themselves and hide (Gen.

3:6-13) from the presence of the Lord God. God saw and supplied the immediate needs of both Adam and the woman.

The curse is noted. After the curse, Adam called his wife's name Eve because she was the mother (v. 20) of all living. God made coats of skin (v. 21), and clothed them. It is conceivable to conclude that an animal or animals were slain. A divinely provided garment was made to cover the nakedness (v. 7) of both Adam and his wife Eve, that our first parents (sinners) were made presentable (fit) for the presence of the Lord God. These divinely provided garments for Adam and his wife Eve (v. 21) relates to an event as parallels to Christ-The first sacrifice is announced.

Through the eyes and the mind of the spiritually discerned, one is able to perceive the crimson blood of the slain beast (v. 21) as it flows and stands coagulated upon the dust of the ground and about the body of the blameless beast. The aprons of (Gen. 3:7) fig leaves were sewed together as a covering to hide their unworthiness, which did not or could not be sufficient. According to God's purpose and plan: "Sin is disobedience to God's law." The aprons of fig leaves were sewed by earthly hands. Through divine inception, God made (divinely provided garments) coats of skins, covering over the disgrace and the nakedness of both Adam and his wife. The crimson blood from the innocent animal is noted. Because of sin, an innocent animal was slain (Job. 29:14).

It is possible that both Adam and his wife Eve viewed the shedding of crimson blood as it flowed from the body of the moveless beast, timely saturating the dust of the ground.

The Scripture (Gen. 2:19-20) tells us that Adam was divinely authorized to give names to every living creature, "that was the name thereof...." It is possible, one might conclude rationally, that both Adam and his wife Eve rationally observed the animal silently that was slain, with fixed eyes, possibly expressing profound concentration of the human results-the consequences (Rom. 3:23, 5:12-14, 6:23) of his sin. By divine authority, the first promise (Gen. 3:15) of a Redeemer is noted. Redemption was essential to save the world. Again, God was always in the knowledge and foreknowledge of all things. God purposed a redemptive plan to save us from sin and death (Eph. 1:4-5). "From Genesis to Revelation...Christ is the theme, the key to the Holy Bible."

Again, God is life, the only source of life. God is the breath of all humankind, whose footsteps are made possible only by the power and the grace of God. "Thou art worthy, O Lord, to receive glory and honor and power: for thou hast created all things, and for thy pleasure they are and were created." (Rev. 4:11)

The Effects of Transgression and Iniquity

Webster's Dictionary defines transgression as the breaking or violating of any law. The Bible tells us transgression is a violation of God's law-disobedience and disbelief transgress God's law. Please note: (Gen. 3:1-13; 4:1-9; 10-15; Num. 20:9-12; 23-24; Jonah 1:1-3). Indeed, our first parents did transgress the Divine command of God (Gen. 3:6). Iniquity is defined as lack of justice or righteousness. The Bible tells us, "Iniquity is the depth of sin," "All unrighteousness (I John 5:17)...is sin...," and "God's Divine Sacrifice for sin will be related."

Let us note the contrast between good and evil, right and wrong (Gen. 4:1-13). Abel was a keeper of sheep. Cain, his brother, was a tiller of the ground. "Cain was satisfied to bring as an offering unto the Lord-the fruit that had fallen upon the ground...which was of bloodless substance-without Divine meaning." Cain's offering reflected the rejection of God's Divine way. "The life of the flesh...is in the blood..." (Lev. 17:11; Heb. 9:22). "Abel brought unto the Lord the very best that he had to offer as a sin offering." "By faith Abel sacrificed unto the Lord of the firstlings (lambs) of his flock." "...Without shedding of blood is no remission..." (Heb. 9:22). The blood is the essence of life. Abel's offering was a sacrifice of excellence unto the Lord. Cain's offering was not acceptable unto the Lord. He was filled with wroth (very angry) and envy because Abel's offering was a more excellent sacrifice unto the Lord. The Scripture tells us, "They were in the field...Cain rose up against Abel (his brother)...and slew him...." Indeed, we can perceive good and evil. Cain's gift was evil-without Divine meaning. Abel's gift was righteous in the eyes of God according to the known will of God. "All unrighteousness...is sin...." (I John 5:17).

Both Adam and Eve did transgress the Divine command of God (Gen. 3:6). The effects from the infraction of God's law passed from generations. "For until the law...sin was in the world...." "Nevertheless...death reigned from Adam to Moses...." (Rom. 5:13-14). Indeed, sin aspires one to act or react in a wicked manner. Satan is the source of unrighteousness. "For from the heart...come evil thoughts...." Again, the remedy for sin will be related (atonement).

From the descendants of our first parents (Adam and his wife Eve), their sons Cain, Seth, and their families, the population grew rapidly on the earth (Gen. 4:-5:). The generations multiplied into great numbers. The Scripture tells us, "...And hath made of one blood (Acts 17:26)....all nations of men for to dwell on all the face of the earth...."

It is wise to note the difference between what is good and what is evil, what is right and what is wrong in the eyes of God. Because of the wickedness (Gen. 6:1, 7) of man, the earth was filled with violence and corruption--all flesh had corrupted his way upon the entire earth. "God saw the wickedness of man...that every imagination of the thought of his heart was only evil continually...." And it repented the Lord that He had made man on the earth and it grieved Him at His heart. Indeed, one can perceive the fact-disobedience is always deeply deploring at the heart of God.

"And the Lord said...I will destroy man whom I have created from the face of the earth...." From the generations of mankind God found only one just and perfect man. "But Noah found grace in the eyes of the Lord." Noah was perfect in his generations. He was a preacher of righteousness, and he walked with God. Day by day, Noah lived and observed the violence and corruption existing from generation to generation, nonetheless, Noah remained righteous, obedient in perfect fellowship with God at all times.

And God said unto Noah, "The end of all flesh is come before me...I will destroy them with the earth...." God told Noah to make thee an ark. God instructed Noah as to the fashion of the ark. Noah was wholly in obedience to God-he followed all of God's instructions. During the age of violence and corruption, Noah was constantly relating to the people the righteousness of God, making them aware of God's Divine existence, and God's Divine presence at all times.

It is a fact that God is sovereign and His Word is infallible. God demands of us fervent acknowledgment of His Divine existence, His presence, and His sovereignty at all times, also the utmost zeal to willingly obey His Word, no matter where we are nor the circumstances in our midst.

During the building of the ark it is possible, and quite conceivable, because of disbelief amid the people Noah was constantly questioned or derided concerning his steadfast spiritual beliefs and his sincere endeavors to God before and while he was preparing the ark as a refuge for the preservation of life. Nevertheless, Noah would not be deterred. It took Noah one hundred and twenty years to build the ark. Noah was determined to obey the will, and the way of God, regardless of the wavering opinions expressed by the people. Indeed, the people had more than ample time to rectify their lives and live in accordance to the laws of God, but like sheep, they wondered in footsteps of wickedness for generations.

Noah was a righteous servant expounding the precepts of God, which he repeatedly emphasized in the midst of the people as factual testimony. God was going to send a flood to destroy the whole earth-all that had breath, and every living substance was going to be destroyed from the face of the earth. Still, the people continued in their wicked folly. They did not consider Noah's testimony to be factual. God purposed a plan to preserve the future of the human race. "And of every living thing of all flesh-two of every sort shall thou bring into the ark...they shall be male and female...." Finely, according to the Divine will of God, the ark was completed.

"And the Lord said unto Noah...Come thou and all thy house into the ark...." In the selfsame day entered Noah, and Shem, and Ham, and Ja'-pheth, the sons of Noah, and Noah's wife and the three wives of his sons with them, into the ark; "...and the Lord shut him in....And the flood was forty days upon the earth...and bare up the ark, and it was lifted up above the earth...And the ark went upon the face of the waters." All in whose nostrils was the breath of life of all that was in dry land...died.

"And God remembered Noah...and every living thing-and God made a wind to pass over the earth (Gen. 8:1), and the waters assuaged...." The waters abated after the end of the hundred and fifty days. "And the ark rested upon the mountains of Ar'-arat." Noah knew the waters were abated from the earth because the dove he sent forth, "...came back to the ark with an olive leaf in her mouth...The dove was sent forth again...but did not return again unto him...And Noah removed the covering of the ark...and looked...and behold-the face of the ground was dry...."

And God spake unto Noah, saying to go forth of the ark-thou, and thy wife, and thy sons, and thy sons' wives with thee. "...Every living thing of all flesh, and every creeping thing after their kind...went forth out of the ark...."

"And Noah builded an altar unto the Lord (vs. 20-22)-and offered burnt offerings (sacrifices) on the altar, as worship unto God." "And the Lord smelled a sweet savor-and the Lord said in his heart...I will not again curse the ground any more for man's sake...."

The universe was replenished by those that were sheltered in the ark-purposed and controlled by the sovereign Spirit power of the Almighty God. According to the scripture (I Pet. 3:20-21), eight souls were saved by the water. God established an everlasting covenant (Gen. 9:8-17) with Noah, and his seed after him.

The descendants of the sons of Noah multiplied rapidly, overspreading the earth. The population increased from tribes, cities, and countries into great nations, their habitation was scattered upon the face of all the earth. Noah was nine hundred and fifty years, and he died.

"Abram, who was a descendant of Shem's line...was called by the Lord, he was sent out of the country (Gen. 12:1-4) on a precise journey...." Abram did not question the call of the Lord. He made immediate plans and departed on his way, unaware where he was going, nor did he know the distance of his assigned (Heb. 11:8) journey. Nevertheless, it appears that Abram had only the thoughts of surety within the realm of his mind. He was wholly trusting, (by faith) leaning on the infallible promises of God to safely direct and guide him as he journeyed on his way (Gen. 12:1-9) by day, and by night. Indeed, faith is the gift of God. Faith comes from the heart and faith comes by hearing the Word of God, and believing (Rom. 10:17; Mat. 21:22). "Now faith is the substance of things hoped for-the evidence of things not seen (Heb. 11:1). "Abraham joyed with faith in God."

"And I will make of thee a great nation-and I will bless thee-and make thy name great-and thou shalt be a blessing." Indeed, Abram's heart and mind did not appear to be centered within the realm of the word maybe, "...because he was not wavering, doubting the promises of God. Abram possessed, and maintained a delivering faith in God (11:8). In the Old Testament, the word faith is noted in the books of (Deut. 32:20; Hab. 2:4). The fathers (servants of God) loved, trusted, feared, and obeyed God. Webster's Dictionary defines trust as faith, belief, confidence, and dependence. Please note: (Rom. 4:13-25; Gal. 3:16-29).

The land of Canaan was promised to Abram, and his seed after him. Abram encountered a grievous famine in the land-still, he continued on the pilgrimage of his assigned mission. Abram experienced pondering moments concerning his wife and his life, "Abram's wife was a fair woman to look upon-she was commended before Pharaoh, ...and the woman was taken into Pharaoh's house...." Indeed, God is in the knowledge of all things. "And the Lord plagued Pharaoh and his house with great plagues, because of Sarai, ... Abram's wife." Abram advised his wife Sarai to tell the Egyptians that she was his sister (Gen. 12:10-20). Sarai was represented as Abram's sister. "Upon Abram's return to Canaan, he returned to the place of the altar...and called on the name of the Lord...." (Gen. 13:4).

Abram was a man of complete faith (Heb. 11:8; 17), also Sarai, Abram's wife. They believed on the promises and the prophecies of the Lord (Gen. 15:). "And Abram said, Lord God-what wilt thou give me...seeing I go childless....?" God promised a heir to Abram; he believed in the promises of the Lord; and the Lord counted it to him for righteousness. In the same day (v.18) the Lord made a covenant with Abram.

Abram fathered a son (Gen. 16:) by Hagar the handmaid, his name was Ishmael. The Scripture reveals contention (Gen. 21:9-12) between Sarai and the handmaid. The Lord was in the knowledge of the immediate needs of both Hagar and her child-the Lord made provisions for their future. The child was circumcised at age thirteen. It is a fact that "all of the plans, and all of the purposes of the Lord God have been Divinely established, ...and will come to pass...."

The sign (Gen. 17:) of the Abrahamic covenant is noted. "Abraham was ninety years old and nine...when he was circumcised...." Please note (Gen.17:24). We note the covenants (a binding and solemn agreement as promises), noting back to (Gen. 12:1-3; Gal. 3:6-18). "In thee shall all the families of the earth be blessed." Let us note these Scriptures: Gen. 3:15, the seed of the woman; Gen. 12:1-3, the promised seed (Gal. 3:16); Gen. 22:18; Acts 3: 25; Gen. 12;3. "And if ye be Christ's-then are ye Abraham's seed-and heirs according to the promise."

Abram's name was changed (Gen. 17:) to Abraham. Sarai's name was changed to Sarah. God promised Abraham and Sarah a son. Abraham fell upon his face and laughed, questioning the fact of a child as he was one hundred years old and his wife Sarah was ninety years old. "And thou shalt call his name Isaac: and I will establish my covenant with him for an everlasting covenant-and with his seed after him." The promise was reaffirmed to Abraham and Sarah by three angels that visited Abraham (Gen. 18:).

Wickedness is noted in the cities of the plain. The cities were destroyed (Gen. 19:) because the inhabitants of the cities were wicked (sinful). Abraham witnessed as God destroyed Sodom and Gomorrah. "But the men of Sodom were wicked and sinners before the Lord exceedingly." The declaring of condemnation noted (II Pet. 2:2-10). Let us note back: Nimrod built the city Babel and a tower, purposely to magnify man. The ideas of the people were vain (Gen. 11:1-9). "The name of the Lord is a strong tower."

Abraham is still on his assigned journey traveling toward the south country. He met with Abimlech saying of his wife Sarah, "She is my sister, and Abimlech, the king of Gerar, sent and took Sarah. Indeed, there are no secrets with God, "...and be sure your sins will find you out...." God was in the foreknowledge of Abraham's deception, "But God came to Abimlech in a dream by night, and said to him-Behold-thou art but a dead man-for the woman which thou hast taken-for she is a man's wife." Even Sarah said, "...He is my brother...."

Abraham was a man of prayer. He returned unto the altar and there he called on the name of the Lord. The mark of deception (Gen. 27:) is noted in Jacob's past. The Scripture (32:24-32) tells us that Jacob wrestled with an angel. David was chosen by God (I Sam. 16:1, 13). David violated (II Sam. 11:1-27) God's law and David confessed with sorrow (I John 1:8-10) his transgression unto the Lord (repented). "The fervent prayers availeth much."

Before creation (Is. 57:15; Rom. 8:28-31), God knew the weakness (Mat. 26:41) of the flesh, "...and God was aware of each individual's capabilities and instabilities." The path of man's footsteps are known by God (Ps. 139:3). The Scripture tells us, "Ponder the path of thy feet-and let all thy ways be established (Prov. 4:26)."

Because of the fall of man in the garden of Eden, we were all made sinners (Gen. 2:16-17; Gen. 3; Rom. 5:12-14). It is a fact that "Satan is a known deceiver...which deceiveth the whole world...." Indeed, God's love and mercy and His kindness towards mankind is so precious, and profound.

Abraham (the father of true believers) trusted wholly upon God's first promise (Gen. 12:3) of "redemption." God is Sovereign. "...Every purpose of God is established...." Both Abraham and Sarah were living examples believing on the promises and living for the glory of God. "For Sarah conceived, ...and bare Abraham a son in his old age...." Abraham circumcised his son Isaac being eight days old, as God had commanded him (Gen. 21:). "All things are possible with God-only believe." After the birth of Isaac, Sarah asked of Abraham, "Cast out the bondwoman-and her son Ishmael." Abraham grievously (vs. 9-21) hearkened unto Sarah's voice. Hagar (the handmaid), and Ishmael were sent away. Indeed, God was aware of the needs of both Hagar, and her son Ishmael-God made provisions for their future.

The faith of Abraham was tested. God commanded Abraham to go into the land of Moriah, "...and offer his son (Isaac) there for a burnt offering upon one of the mountains referred to him by God...." Again, Abraham did not question God's command. Immediately, he made plans to go to the specified place which God had appointed him, "and he saw the place afar off...." Indeed, Isaac questioned his father's actions and he said, "Behold the fire...and the wood: but where is the lamb for the burnt offering?" Indeed, Abraham (Gen. 22:1-19) built an altar to offer (sacrifice) his son Isaac upon the altar as a burnt offering (vs. 9-12), but God provided (v.13) for Abraham. Please note (v. 18; Acts 3:25); it is a fact that man must completely surrender to God's established way and walk in the spiritual pathway to please God.

Sarah died in the faith. Sarah was a hundred and twenty seven years old-these were the years of the life of Sarah (the princess-a woman of faith) (Gen. 23:1).

Abraham secured a wife for his son Isaac. Her name was Rebekah, she was the mother of Esau and Jacob. Abraham married Keturah and begot other children. Abraham gave all that he had unto Isaac, Sarah's son. "The sons of the concubines-which Abraham had-Abraham gave gifts...and sent them away from Isaac...."

Abraham died in the faith. Abraham lived a hundred threescore and fifteen years (175 years old). Abraham and Sarah were buried in the field which Abraham purchased from sons of Heth for possession of a burying place. They were buried in the cave of the field of Machpelah before Mamre, the same is Hebron in the land of Canaan. "The patriarchs are buried there." Abraham was totally aware that "...there was an Eternal city of the living God-which was prepared for the saints." For Abraham looked for a city which hath foundations, whose builder and maker was God.

Looking back through the tunnel scope of time, perceiving the miraculous realities of God, noting the perfected wonders and the unchanging beauties surrounding God's (handiworks) creations. Indeed, there should be little or no wondering why we periodically ponder and vision back into the beginning of creation, recognizing and immediately sanctioning, without wavering, the Divine existence of God and the Divine sovereignty of God.

The first created man was Adam-created in the image of the Lord God (Gen. 1:26-27, 2:7). God promised Adam a Savior (Gen. 3:15), the seed of the woman. Adam was called the son of God (Luke 3:38). The fall of man is noted because of man's disobedience to God's command (Rom. 5:12-19). Let us note, "And hath made of one blood all nations of men...for to dwell on all the face of the earth...."

Gen. 5 relates to the genealogies. The ancestral lineage of the patriarchs on the other side of the flood. It is important to note: (Gen. 6:8).

Gen. 6:5-14 relates to the wickedness of mankind before the flood-all forms of evil existed. "But Noah found grace in the eyes of the Lord." I Pet. 3:20 tells us that eight souls were saved by the water. The eight souls were the families of Noah, who was the father and patriarch of the new world, after the flood.

(Gen. 10:) relates to the descendants of the sons of Noah-the origin of nations (v.32). Noah, the head of the race-he was the tenth male in the decent of Adam-in the line of Seth, the third son of Adam.

Noah's sons were Shem, Ham, and Japheth. They shared in the responsibility of replenishing (over-spreading) the human race over the whole earth, noting that Abraham was a descendant of Shem's line, the oldest son of Noah. Please note: (Chr. 1:24-27). The Scripture tells us that Ham was the father of Canaan. The land of Canaan was later promised to Abraham (Gen. 12:,) and his seed (26:2-5).

Looking back through the scope of time-perceiving on this side of the flood-picturing in mind the spiritual aspects of faith, hope, vision, values, and principles that points to the life of Abraham during his adult years while living in his native home in the city of Ur of the Calddees, in the country of Mesopotamia. It is noted that Abraham left Ur of the Calddees to go into the land of Canaan, he came into Haran, and dwelt there. The Scripture tells us Abraham was Divinely called (Gen. 12:).

Abraham was a patriarch, an ancestor of the Hebrews. The patriarchs were sojourners, they were referred to as ancient families or tribal heads (Gen. 18:18-19)-as the Israelites were a branch of the family of Abraham.

In the New Testament, the name "patriarch" applied to the founders of the Hebrew race-nation and a religion. The noted names are: Abraham (Heb. 7:4); the sons of Jacob (Acts 7:8-9); and David (Acts 2:29-30)-noting (II Sam. 7:12-13). The genealogies and the given account of the covenant histories referred to names before Moses' time (Ex. 2:).

The tribes of Israel descended from the sons of Jacob. The tribes (twelve in number) were patriarchs (Acts 7:8-9). And so Abraham begat Isaac, "...Abraham circumcised his son being eight days old...." And Isaac begat Jacob; and Jacob (whose name was changed (Gen. 32:22-32) to Israel) begat the twelve patriarchs. The descendants of Jacob (Israel) were the Israelites that, "...later began as a nation (Ex. 1:) in Egypt." The bondage (vs. 1-22) in Egypt will be related.

Jacob and his brother Esau were reconciled. Esau sold his birthright to his brother Jacob (Gen. 25:). Esau was later deprived of his blessing from his father Isaac and he wept-Here deceitfulness is noted (Gen. 27:). Esau was angry with his brother Jacob. Nonetheless, in due time (Gen. 33:) they embraced, kissed, and they wept. "...For therefore I have seen thy face-as though I had seen the face of God-and thou wast pleased with me...." Isaac was deceived by Jacob (Gen. 27:1-25).

Isaac, the son of Abraham died. The days of Isaac were a hundred and fourscore years. Esau and Jacob buried him in the cave that is in the field of Machpelah in the land of Canaan. Isaac's father Abraham purchased the field from the children of Heth for a burying place.

Let us trace the footsteps of Jacob's sons, perceiving the lives of the twelve patriarchs and noting the following Chapters (37:-50:) Now Israel loved Joseph more than all his children (v. 3) because he was the son of his old age and he made him a coat of many colors. Jacob's favoritism towards Joseph excited his brethren into a state of rage, hate, and jealousy. The brethren were aware that Joseph was a dreamer, and for this "...they were more excited." It is noted (vs. 20-36) that Joseph was stripped out of his coat of many colors by his brethren and cast into a pit. He was sold to the Ishmaelites for twenty pieces of silver, and brought into Egypt. "Joseph was stolen away...out of the land of the Hebrews." The deceptive actions of the brethren revealed to us the effects of/from the aversion within their hearts. Mat. 15:19 tells us, For out of the heart...proceed evil thoughts." After their pit decision of Joseph they uttered, "...And we shall see what will become of his dreams." Indeed, God was aware of Joseph's dreams.

From day to day in Egypt, Joseph did not appear to be angered or perplexed with his profound faith in God-he could perceive, recognizing the factual prophecies, and the promises of God, "Fear thou not-for I am with thee: be not dismayed-for I am thy God: I will strengthen thee-yea-I will help thee-yea, I will uphold thee with the right hand of my righteousness." (Is. 41:10). Joseph was aware of the fact that "...he had put on the whole armor of God-and taken on the shield of faith...." Joseph was also aware that "...God had preceded his footsteps-and every purpose of God is established-and can not be annulled."

Joseph advanced rapidly in the house of his master the Egyptian. It was noted by his master that "...God was with Joseph." The Lord made all that he did to prosper in his hand. The Lord blessed the Egyptian's house (39:-41:) for Joseph's sake-and the blessing of the Lord was upon all that he had in the house-and in the field.

Joseph was falsely accused (vs. 7-23) without cause. False accusations are noted in our midst today. It is possible that "...the painful memories of these occurrences abide within the minds of the innocent indefinitely." All injustice is knowledgable to God. "...For the Lord is a God of knowledge...."

It is possible, and quite conceivable that Joseph's mind periodically wondered back, unraveling thoughts of memorable moments appearing like striking images due to the accusations indicated by Potiphar's wife. Joseph was put in prison-the king's prisoners were bound there. "But the Lord was with Joseph, and showed him mercy-and gave him favor in the sight of the keeper of the prison."

It is a fact that no matter when, nor where, we yield to intervene as partakers by deceptive means towards others, let us stop and ponder, let us examine ourselves. God is aware of all of our deeds. Indeed, God imparts to his children that needed strength, the needed courage to love and the faith to pray with hope for our enemies "while He gently directs the footsteps of those that love, and trust in Him without wavering."

Let us note that "...God was in the foreknowledge of Joseph's plight before he was born" while the brethren and his master rejected him by deceptive means. God's plan and purpose for Joseph's being was Divinely established.

It is not difficult for true believers to perceive God's concern (Ps. 105:16-20) and His purpose for the preservation of His people. We will note that the lives of the people in Egypt were preserved by the power of God through the works of Joseph. I Cor.

12:6 tells us, "And there are diversities of operations-but it is the same God which worketh all in all."

Joseph understood dreams (Gen. 40:-41:). He interpreted the dreams of the chief butler and the dreams of the chief baker. And Joseph said to them, "Do not interpretations belong to God?" Joseph acknowledged the fact that "...Every good gift and every perfect gift is from above." The butler nor the baker had acquired the true knowledge about the Sovereign God-they only identified themselves with the Egyptian deities (the worshipping of idols). Nevertheless, without choice, both the butler and the baker believed in Joseph's interpretations. It is noted that "...Joseph's interpretations come true." Joseph related to the chief butler, "But think on me when it shall be well with thee-and show kindness-I pray thee, unto me-and make mention of me unto Pharaoh-and bring me out of this house for indeed-I was stolen away ...out of the land of the Hebrews."

II Cor. 4:8 tells us that we are troubled on every side, yet not distressed. We are perplexed, but not in despair. God was in the foreknowledge of the obstacles that would befall Joseph, the exact time and place. It is through the Divine operation of God's Spirit power that "...mankind is given specified strength (noting Is. 41:10) to overcome the snares that lie ahead in the path of life." Joseph was a man of faith, and God was there sustaining him, lifting him above all the pitfalls. I Cor. 10:13 tells us, "There hath no temptation taken you but such as is common to man: but God is faithful-who will not suffer you to be tempted above that ye are able; but will with the temptation also make a way to escape-that ye may be able to bear it." For indeed, "...God is a buckler to all that trust in Him." Let us note, "perceiving the 'Sovereignty' of God's hand in human occurrences."

Gen. 41:1-13 tells us that at the end of two full years Pharaoh dreamed. And it came to pass that, "...Pharaoh was troubled in spirit." Pharaoh was a noted king, the ruler of Egypt. Why did Pharaoh's mind fall into a profound state of mystification? The king did not understand the anxieties that had troubled him after his dreams. The striking life-like images continued to annoy Pharaoh, he sent and called for the magicians of Egypt and all the wise men thereof, "...nevertheless, there was none that could interpret Pharaoh's dreams...."

The news was acquired by Pharaoh that "...there was a Hebrew servant to the captain of the guard-and all of his interpretations were factual." Pharaoh sent and called Joseph and they brought him hastily out of the dungeon and he shaved himself and changed his raiment, and came in unto Pharaoh (vs. 14-36). And Pharaoh said unto Joseph, "I have dreamed a dream, and there is none...that can interpret it." Joseph made known to Pharaoh the factual source of his understanding of dreams to interpret them. It is not in me, "God shall give Pharaoh an answer of peace." Indeed, the Sovereignty of God can be perceived as factual, and the promises of God are unfailing. "He will be our guide...even unto death...." Through the Divine works of God, Joseph (the Hebrew servant) was making footsteps out of the dungeon never to be hurt again with the fetters as he was laid in iron (Ps. 105:16-21.)

Joseph related, explaining the facts to Pharaoh according to his understanding of the interpretation of his dreams: "Behold, there come seven years of great plenty throughout all the land of Egypt." And there shall arise after them seven years of famine; and all the plenty shall be forgotten in the land of Egypt; and the famine shall consume the land; "...And the plenty shall not be known in the land...." By faith,

Joseph was eagerly looking forward to the seven years of plenty followed by seven years of famine. "It is because the thing is established...by God-and God will shortly bring it to pass...." noting Gen. 41:25-31. Joseph subjected the approval of appointed officers over the land (overseers) that "...the land perish not through the famine...."

Pharaoh recognized and acknowledged the fact that "...Joseph was influenced (vs. 37-57) by an invisible Supernal power...." Pharaoh made Joseph ruler over his house, and ruler over all the land of Egypt. Joseph was thirty years old when he stood before Pharaoh.

During the seven plenteous years, Joseph laid up food in every city. Joseph gathered corn as the sand of the sea, "...for it was without number...."

Looking back, let us note, it is possible, and quite conceivable, the brethren had assumed they had accomplished their plight to rid themselves of Joseph (the master of dreams) never to see his face again. Joseph was sold to the Ishmaelites for twenty pieces of silver and brought into Egypt (Gen. 37:18-36).

The years of plenty ended in the land of Egypt. The famine was over the face of the earth. And all countries came into Egypt to Joseph to buy corn because the famine was sore in all the land of Egypt. Joseph opened all the storehouses, "...because the famine was very bad...."

Now when Jacob (Joseph's father) saw that there was corn in Egypt, Jacob said unto his sons, "Why do ye look one upon another?" Jacob sent ten of his sons to buy corn in Egypt. But Benjamin, Joseph's brother, Jacob sent not with the brethren (Gen. 42-44). Let us note that Jacob was not aware that "...Joseph (his favorite son) was still alive...." However, it is possible when the brethren heard their father relate to them their need for food, and that they must go into Egypt to buy corn, they were reminded of their past activities at the pit and they were also concerned about the false report they had given to their father Jacob concerning the absence of their brother Joseph (Gen. 37:26-33).

Joseph was the governor over all the land, "...and he sold corn to all the people of the land." Joseph's brethren came to buy corn and Joseph knew them. But they knew him not. The brethren explained to Joseph that the twelve sons belong to one man in the land of Canaan," "...the youngest is this day with our father and the other is not...." The brethren came into Egypt to buy corn, but it appeared that Joseph longed to see his brother Benjamin whom he loved so dearly. The brethren were imprisoned as spies. Send one of you and let him fetch (Gen. 42:14-38) your brother, and ye shall be kept in prison that your words may be proved-whether there be any truth in you, or else by the life of Pharaoh surely ye are spies. And he put them all together into ward three days.

And Joseph said unto them the third day, "This do and live-for I fear God." The brethren noted their treatment from Joseph when he besought them and they discussed the pass (Gen. 37:21) among themselves. And they knew not that Joseph understood them for he spake unto them by an interpreter. "And he turned himself about...from them-and he wept-and returned to them again, and communed with them, and took from them Simeon-and bound him before their eyes." Then Joseph commanded to fill their sacks with corn, and to restore every man's money into his sack. And they laded their asses with the corn, and departed thence. The men discovered, "...their money was returned, and they were afraid...." And they came unto

Jacob their father unto the land of Canaan, and told him all that befell unto them, saying, "The man who is the lord of the land, spake roughly to us, and took us for spies of the country."

The men related unto their father Jacob (v.34) the request of the man "...who is the lord of the land...." Jacob gave his approval (vs. 13-15) to let Benjamin go with the brethren down in Egypt. Simeon was already held as hostage by Joseph. And the famine was sore in the land (Gen. 43:). And Judah said unto Israel his father, "...Send the lad with me, and I will arise and go-that we may live-and not die, both we, and thou, and also our little ones." And the men took that present, and they took double money in their hand, and Benjamin, and rose up, and went down to Egypt and stood before Joseph. And when Joseph saw Benjamin with them, he said to the ruler of his house, "Bring these men home-and make ready-for these men shall dine with me at noon." The men were brought into Joseph's house, "...and the men were afraid...." The men communed with the steward of Joseph's house, at the door of the house. They were concerned, "...because their money for food, had been returned in the sack's mouth...." And he said, "Peace be with you, fear not: your God, and the God of your father, hath given you treasure in your sacks: I had your money." And he brought Simeon out unto them.

And when Joseph came home, they brought him the present which was in their hand into the house, and bowed themselves to him to the earth. The steward had prepared the brethren for the reunion (v. 24;), and he gave their asses provender. God had made possible, the coming together of Jacob's sons known as (Acts 7:8;-13;) the twelve patriarchs. Of Israel, the descendants of "Abraham," the father of many nations.

The brethren were face to face with Joseph (Gen. 43:27-34) as he proceeded to inquire about their welfare and the health of their father. "...Is he yet alive?" Thy servant our father is in good health, "...he is yet alive...." During the reunion, Joseph's eyes were intentively fixed upon Benjamin. A striking resemblance (35:17-18) brought back memories of the past, "...and he sought where to weep; and he entered into his chamber, and wept there...." Joseph and Benjamin were Rachel's sons. Joseph refrained himself and said, "...Set on the bread...."

The noonday meal was prepared, and set on for Joseph by himself, and for the brethren by themselves. The Egyptians, who did eat with him, were seated by themselves. The conception, or the opinion of the Egyptians (43:32; 46:34), is noted. It is considered an abomination unto the Egyptians to eat with aliens (Hebrews), strangers.

Joseph continued his unique intervals of masquerading: He had succeeded in his plights of testing, and had made himself unfamiliar to his brethren; nevertheless, special attention (v. 34) and favors were rendered towards Benjamin.

After the feast (noonday meal), Joseph informed the steward in secrecy to fill the men's sacks with food, and return every man's money in his sack's mouth. The steward was ordered by Joseph to put his silver cup in the sack's mouth of the youngest, and his corn money (Gen. 44:).

When the morning was light, the brethren were sent away, they and their asses. Joseph was aware that "...the brethren were to return unto him." The men were a short distance out of the city, and not yet far off, Joseph commanded the steward to follow after them. They were accused of stealing the priceless silver cup out of the lord's house. The brethren could not prove their guiltlessness, still, they knew they were innocent (v.16). Then they speedily took down every man his sack to the ground, and opened every man his sack. The cup was found in the sack's mouth of Benjamin, just as Joseph had planned (v.2).

The men returned back to the city again, to face the "lord of the country." It is possible, and very conceivable that "...the brethren's minds were retracing (Gen. 37:18-34) back to their deceptive deed at the pit, also the perceiving of a striking image that was left in the pit (vs. 24-28)...."

And Judah and his brethren came to Joseph's house, for he was yet there and they fell before him on the ground. Joseph desired to retain only Benjamin as his servant, the brethren were free (Gen. 44:17) to return back to Canaan unto their father Jacob. Nevertheless, they refused to return unto their father without Benjamin (vs. 30-34). "For how shall I go up to my father-and the lad be not with me? Lest peradventure I see the evil that shall come on my father." Judah offered himself to abide as a bond-man unto the Lord, "...while pleading for Benjamin to go up with his brethren unto his father Jacob: he offered himself as a ransom for Benjamin...." (Please note: v. 16; Gen. 44:33-34).

The conclusion of Joseph's masquerading and the testing of his brethren ends, nevertheless, noting early in the Chapter (39:9), Joseph acknowledged the fact that "...God is the Rock, and His ways, and His works are perfect...." Joseph was a man of faith in God. Joseph's spiritual task required abstaining from wickedness (vs. 10-20) and Joseph fulfilled the task of bearing up the name of God before all mankind that "...the Divine power, and the Divine works of God might be observed through his life, and the endeavors of his works might be an example-as God has purposes for all mankind; yielding, and obeying God's will, and God's way."

Again, Joseph was rejected, kidnapped, and stolen away out of the land of the Hebrews. Let us note that the brethren cast Joseph into the pit. Joseph was alone in the pit in the wilderness. The Midianites passed, and they drew and lifted up Joseph out of the pit and sold Joseph to the Ishmaelites for twenty pieces of silver, and they brought Joseph into Egypt (Gen. 37:23-28). The Midianites were the descendants of Midian, descendants of Abraham by his wife Keturah. The Ishmaelites were descendants of Abraham's son Ishmael, Hagar was his mother. Potiphar, an officer of Pharaoh, captain of the guard, an Egyptian, bought Joseph from the Ishmaelites. "And his master saw that the Lord was with him-and that the Lord made all that he did to prosper in his hand (Gen. 39:3)." Joseph was rejected by his own brethren, nevertheless, his love for them was unchanged.

Amid the brethren, Joseph appeared unbent-ready to make known (42:7; 30-32) a secret unto his brethren that "...brought back memories of the past."

Then Joseph could not refrain (Gen. 45:) himself before all them that stood by him and he cried, "Cause every man to go out from me." And there stood no man with him while Joseph made himself known to his brethren. Indeed, Joseph was emotionally overcome, "...and he wept aloud...." And Joseph said unto his brethren, "I am Joseph; doth my father yet live?" The brethren were troubled (45:3) and could not answer, "...for they were disturbed at Joseph's presence-noting back to their deceptive deed (37:21-36) in the wilderness...." It is conceivable that "...the facial expressions of the brethren were noted by Joseph." Speaking now in his native Hebrew tongue with much compassion Joseph said unto his brethren, "Come near to me-I pray you." And they came near. And he said, "I am Joseph your brother-whom ye sold into Egypt." Joseph did not want his brethren to be grieved, nor did he want them to be angry with themselves, that they had sold him into Egypt. "...for God did send me before you to preserve life...." Noting (vs. 6-8). Indeed, many lives were saved by the great deliverance of God, through the works of Joseph. Noting (Gen. 41:54-57). The works of God were established according to His Divine will, and according to His Divine purpose. "God is sovereign." "For the Lord of host hath purposed-and who shall disannul it? And His hand is stretched out upon all the nations."

Joseph was now awaiting the happy moments to reunite with his father Jacob. Joseph invited, and sent for Jacob to come to Egypt.

"Haste ye-and go up to my father-and say to him-Thus saith thy son Joseph-God hath made me lord of all Egypt: come down unto me-tarry not." (Gen. 45:9-28).

The sight of his brother Benjamin fulfilled one of his greatest desires. Joseph fell upon Benjamin's neck, and they wept together. Joseph kissed all his brethren, and wept upon them and after that his brethren talked with him. Pharaoh and his servants were pleased well when they heard the news that "...the brethren were there." Pharaoh offered the best of everything (vs. 17-20) for Jacob, the brethren, and their households. And the children of Israel did so and Joseph gave them wagons, according to the commandment of Pharaoh, and gave them provision for the way. Again, Joseph sent his brethren away, this time they were sent away prepared to bring back their father Jacob, and his seed into Egypt to dwell in the land of Goshen.

The brethren went up out of Egypt and came into the land of Canaan unto Jacob their father, "And told him-saying-Joseph is yet alive-and he is governor over all the land of Egypt." And Jacob's heart fainted for he believed them not (v. 26; Luke 24:11, 41). The brethren related all the words of Joseph to their father. Indeed, the words of the brethren were pleasing to Jacob, "...and when he saw the wagons which Joseph had sent to carry him-his spirit was revived...." And Jacob said, "...I will go and see him before I die...." Jacob welcomed the thought of reuniting with Joseph, his favorite son.

And Israel took the journey with all that he had, and came to Beersheba, and offered sacrifices unto the God of his father Isaac (Gen. 46). Noting back to Gen. 32:28-30, Jacob's name was changed to Israel. The sons of Israel carried Jacob their father, and their little ones, and their wives in the wagons which Pharaoh had sent to carry him. His sons, and his son's sons with him, his daughters, and his son's daughters, and all his seed brought he with him into Egypt. Judah led Jacob his father into the land of Goshen. And Joseph made ready his chariot and went up to meet Israel his father to Goshen, and presented himself unto him and he fell on his neck and wept on his neck a good while. And Israel said unto Joseph, "Now let me die-since I have seen thy face-because thou art yet alive." Noting back to (Gen. 37:31-32).

Pharaoh was aware that Jacob, the brethren, and their families had moved from the land of Canaan into Egypt, they brought all their goods, and all their cattle with them into the country of Goshen (Gen. 47). Joseph presented some of his brethren unto Pharaoh. And Joseph brought in Jacob his father, and set him before Pharaoh. Jacob blessed Pharaoh and went out from before Pharaoh.

Joseph's endeavors were living examples of sincerity, stableness, caring, forgiving, and spiritual sensitiveness is noted (Gen. 37:2). Joseph recognized and acknowledged the difference between good and evil, noting what is right and what is wrong. Faith was a living reality in Joseph's life.

Joseph gave his father and his brethren a possession in the land of Egypt. They were given the best of the land, "...in the land of Rameses as Pharaoh had commanded...."

Jacob lived in the land of Egypt seventeen years. It is noted that "...their possessions grew-and multiplied exceedingly," noting (v. 11). The whole age of Jacob was a hundred forty and seven years. The time and the days were approaching. Israel felt the need, desiring to confer with Joseph that he might relate, unfolding his wishes to him. And Israel called Joseph and said, "...bury me not-I pray thee-in Egypt.... But I will lie with my fathers-and thou shalt carry me out of Egypt-and bury me in their burying place." And he said, "I will do as thou hast said." Joseph gave his solemn promise to the conveyance of his father's wishes "noting that Joseph was his father's favorite son."

Joseph was told that his father was sick, "...and he took with him his two sons-Manasseh and Ephraim...." Israel was pleased that Joseph and his sons had come unto him. And Israel said unto Joseph, "I had not thought to see thy face: and-lo-God hath showed me thy seed." The sons of Joseph were born in Egypt, before patriarch Jacob moved to Egypt. They were adopted (Gen. 48:1-6) by the patriarch after his moving to Egypt.

Let us note that Jacob's name (Gen. 32:28; 35:9-12) was changed from Jacob to Israel noting that the patriarch was one of the holy prophets (II Pet.1: 20-21), a man of God with steadfast faith, blessed with perceptive power, and prophetic vision relating to Israel's future as a nation.

Israel desired to bless Joseph (Gen. 48:14-16), and his sons. The bestowal of the birthright blessing (v. 16-20) is noted. And Israel stretched out his right hand and laid it upon Ephraim's head, who was the younger, and his left hand upon Manasseh's head, guiding his hands wittingly for Manasseh was the firstborn.

And he blessed Joseph and said,

"God-before whom my fathers Abraham and Isaac did walk, the God who fed me all my life long unto this day, the angel which redeemed me from all evil-bless the lads (Gen. 48:15-16) and let my name be named on them-and the name of my fathers Abraham and Isaac (Gen. 48:20-21)-and let them grow into a multitude in the midst of the earth.

Israel was wholly aware of his actions verbally, and the manner that he exercised his hands upon the lad's heads, noting (Gen. 48:14). The activation, and the sanctioning of the birthright blessing was ratified by Israel, whose name was changed from Jacob to Israel. The name Israel (v. 16) was surrendered by Israel, sealed and passed on upon the sons of Joseph conjointly. The confirming of the birthright blessing upon the lads was sealed indefinitely. Indeed, the name "Israel" was incessantly confirmed upon the sons of Joseph and their descendants. Please note: (I Chr. 5:1-2).

It is conceivable that Israel's inspired visions came by Divine inspirations. The final benediction (Gen. 48:20), and the predictions of Israel clearly point toward the future prospectives of the lads. The individuality, and the separation of the lads was prophetically visioned, and focused upon by Israel, noting that he was going to die.

And he blessed them that day saying, "In thee shall Israel bless" saying, "God make thee as Ephraim and as Manasseh: and he set Ephraim before Manasseh.

Israel concluded the benediction (Gen. 48:15; 16; 20) upon Joseph's sons. (Please note: I Chr. 5:1-2).

Jacob unfolds the prophecy (49:1-27) concerning his sons-They were the twelve tribes of Israel, "...and he blessed them-every one according to his blessing he blessed them...." Let us note that The Messiah was promised through Judah (Gen. 49:10), "From the tribe of Judah." (Heb. 7:14) (Luke 3:33).

Jacob realized his earthly life was nearing an end. He was a man standing on the promises with steadfast faith in the God of Abraham, and the God of his father Isaac. Jacob's spiritual life, and his spiritual progress will be related.

Jacob felt the desire to repeat his last request unto his sons, known as the twelve patriarchs, the twelve tribes of Israel (vs. 28-33). And when Jacob had made an end of commanding his sons, he gathered up his feet into the bed and yielded up the ghost and was gathered unto his people. Jacob's request was conveyed, "For his sons carried him into the land of Canaan-and buried him in the cave of the field...of Machpelah...." Jacob's life was long (Gen. 47:28).

Joseph returned into Egypt, "...he and his brethren." The brethren were concerned (Gen. 50), they were reminded of all the evil (Gen. 37) which they deceitfully forced upon Joseph at the pit. They fervently sought forgiveness from Joseph. "...And Joseph wept when they spake to him...." The brethren feared retaliation from Joseph, now that their father was dead. And Joseph said unto them, "Fear not: for am I in the place of God. But as for you-ye thought evil against me-but God meant it unto good-to bring to pass-as it is this day-to save much people alive."

The death of the patriarch profoundly touched the heart and soul of Joseph. The Egyptians realized and acknowledged how much the long warm friendship with Jacob meant to them. "...And they mourned with a great and sore lamentation...." The memories of the patriarch will ever hold dear within the hearts and the minds of those that loved him so dearly.

It is conceivable to believe that "...Joseph observed his brethren's need to be comforted, and reassured of his love for them (v. 21)." By faith, Joseph desired that his brethren put their trust in God. And Joseph said unto his brethren, "I die: and God will surely visit you-and bring you out of this land unto the land which he sware to Abraham-to Isaac-and to Jacob." It is noted that Joseph desired and conferred with his brethren, conveying to them his wishes concerning his death, noting the fact that he had lived to be a hundred and ten years old.

And Joseph took an oath of the children of Israel saying, "God will surely visit you-and ye shall carry up my bones from hence." So Joseph died "...and they embalmed him-and he was put in a coffin in Egypt...." Please note: (Gen. 50:25; Ex. 13:19; and Josh. 24:32). The final resting place of Joseph's bones was in Shechem, which is in the land of Canaan.

Joseph was God's purposed agent (41:54-57)-the life preserver to save many people alive.

He (God) sent a man before them-even Joseph-who was sold for a servant (Ps. 105:17-21) whose feet they hurt with fetters. He was laid in iron until the time that his word came-the word of the Lord tried him. The king sent and loosed him, even the ruler of the people, and let him go free. He made him lord of his house and ruler of all his substances.

The recognition and the memory of Joseph's fervent concern to preserve life (Gen. 45:5-8) was credited to his God-given wisdom and guidance, that he might successfully rule over all the land of Egypt as governor. Joseph was highly recognized by the Egyptians. The long acquaintance with the patriarch was cherished by the Egyptians.

It is conceivable to assume that the image of Joseph recollected periodically within the minds of the Egyptians. The preserver of life (Gen. 41:38-57) during the famine in Egypt is a noted attribute for Joseph. The marvelous works of God can be observed everywhere...as factual evidence of His Divine existence, and His Divine presence. It is a fact that Joseph's faith in God (Heb. 11:22) was steadfast. "And Joseph said unto his brethren, I die: and God will surely visit you, and bring you out of this land unto the land which He sware to Abraham, to Isaac, and Jacob."

Joseph solemnly directed (Gen. 50:24-26), "...And ye shall carry up my bones from hence...." out of Egypt into the land (12:1, 7) of promise. The land of Canaan was promised to Abraham (12:1-3) and his seed. Joseph was confident, someday, at God's appointed time, he would rise (I Thes. 4:16-17) with the Saints (Heb. 11:22) in the promised land.

The book of Genesis unfolds historical background and insight that reveals the ancient past. All creation, generation, or origin have been unfoled. The leadership of noted men have been narratively outlined step by step. Adam (Gen. 2:7, 15-17, Gen. 3:), Enoch, Noah, Abraham, Isaac, Jacob, and Joseph. The narrative history of Israel's past is noted.

Summary

Looking back, periodically pondering over the marvelous divine works of creation, wholly aware of the fact that God is indeed the Creator (Gen. 1:1-2, John 1:1-5), the ruler and maker of all (Is. 40:12-31) that exist. God is a Spirit (invisible). God is holy, sovereign, everlasting, omnipotent, omnipresent, and omniscient. God is so real. Indeed, God's grace is sufficient for thee.

God foreknew (Eph. 1:3-12) the weakness of the flesh, wholly aware that man would sin (Gen. 2:17, 3:) and fall in Eden. God was concerned about the souls of men before creation. God was concerned about the souls of men in the ancient times of the creation. It is indeed a fact that God is the same yesterday, and today, and forever. (Ps. 139:1-15).

God is the origin (Gen. 1:1-31) of all creation. God is the origin (Gen. 1:26-28, 2:7, 18-25) of humankind and everything that breathe the breath of life. God is the sole supplier of the air-one of life's necessities. It is impossible to erase the name or debase the living Word of God (Eph. 3:9) as the Source, and the origin of all things. The sovereignty of God should be recognized at all times. God is the Source of evolution. God is the Source of the theories that made the means of evolution (John 1:1-5) possible, noting the unfolding of the process of development, formation or growth.

The Scripture (Gen. 2:7) tells us, "And the Lord God formed man of the dust of the ground, and breathed into his nostrils the breath of life; and man became a living soul." Eccl. 7:29 tells us, "God made man upright, created in a holy state: Created in God's (Gen. 1:27) image. Only the breath (Job 12:10), (Acts 17:25-29) of God giveth life. Let us give God the glory: He is worthy to be praised."

The origin of sin (Gen. 3:1-13) is unfoled. Satan's power and temptation is exercised. The deceit and the craftiness of the beast is noted. The serpent was used as

Satan's tool (Gen. 3:1) to allure and to beguile the woman in Eden. The woman was deceived (I Tim. 2:14); Adam was not deceived; he willingly (Gen. 2:16-17) disobeyed (3:6) God's command. Adam's mind was swayed (influenced) by Satan's power (vs. 1-3). Indeed, God was in the foreknowledge that Satan would intervene as an influencing force to deceive, according to the will, the purpose, and the plan of God. Again, God foreknew that man would fall (3:1-5) in the garden of Eden noting (vs. 6-7); (vs. 8-24). The curse (vs. 14-19) is noted. And Adam called his wife's name Eve because she was the mother of all living. "...God clothed Adam (v. 21), and his wife...."

Sin entered (Rom. 5:12-19) into the world. We were all made sinners (3:23). Redemption was essential (necessary)—God's plan to save a dying world. The promise of the redeemer (Gen. 3:15) is unfold—to pay the ransom (Mat. 20:28), to rectify (Gen. 3:1-24) the fall of man in Eden, and to repurchase (Heb. 9:12, 22) the sinful souls of humankind. Sin separates (Is. 59:2) us from God. Only God and man can change the fall (John 3:16) of man because we are born (Ps. 51:5) in sin. The consequence of man's sin (Gen. 2:17, 3:3) is noted. The effect of sin appears to be actuating (Mat. 15:18-19) throughout the world today.

Looking back into the ages of the past, noting the contrast between Cain's offering, and Abel's offering unto the Lord, Cain's offering was of the fruit of the ground-lifeless and faithless, wholly without type or foreshadow typifying the atonement paralleling to Calvary. Cain was the first son (Gen. 4:1-3) of Adam and Eve. Abel offered an animal (v. 4) sacrifice, a lamb of his flock as an appropriate offering (Gen. 3:15, 22:7-8), (Heb. 11:4) as a sacrifice unto the Lord. The righteous belief of Abel was approved by God-deemed as an excellent sacrifice. The first exemplar (worthy) of God's way of righteousness through faith, noting his obedience unto God. Redemption was God's plan. Redemption is by the blood, and God's grace. The Scripture (Lev. 17:11) tells us, "For the life of the flesh is in the blood. Redemption is salvation by sacrifice, through the promised (Gen. 3:15) Redeemer," noting (Gal. 4:4).

The Scripture (Gen. 6:1-14) tells us that the flood was brought on the earth as a judgment on the sins of the people. "Noah found grace (v. 8) in the eyes of the Lord." Noah (v. 9) walked with God. According to the will of God, "...Every purpose (Prov. 20:18) is established by counsel...at God's appointed time...." The future of humanity is noted. There were eight souls saved (I Pet. 3:20) by water. The families of Noah were responsible (Gen. 10:1-32) for the repopulation and the emerging of humankind over the whole earth, noting (Act 17:26).

The animals and the fowls were specified (Gen. 7:1-4) by demand, according to the specifications of God. The clean animals, and the clean fowls were set apart for divine worship (8:20-21) unto God. The faith of Noah (Heb. 11:7) is noted. Abel's sacrifice (Gen. 4:4) unto God was received, and approved as excellent. The faith of Abel (Heb. 11:4) is noted. Abraham's sacrifice (Gen. 22:1-2; 7-8) unto God, and his steadfast faith (15:6), (Heb. 11:17) in God is noted. "Now faith is the substance of things hoped for, the evidence of things not seen." (Gen. 22:9-18) is noted.

God was wholly in the foreknowledge of our footsteps before the creation (Eph. 1:4-5) of the universe. God is the same yesterday, and today, and forever.

Looking back into the garden of Eden, visioning man's disobedience (Gen. 2:17, 3:6, 19) unto God, sin entered (Rom. 5:12) into the world. We were all made (Rom. 3:23) sinners. The Scripture (Is. 59:2) tells us that Sin separates us from God.

Nonetheless, God loved us while we were yet sinners. God's love for all mankind is eternal. "God hates sin."

The sinful nature of humankind was not destroyed during the flood, the deluge, the great flood (Gen. 7) in the days of Noah. The sinful nature of humankind (Rom. 3:23, 5:12-14) was merely preserved until God's specified time to manifest (reveal) the guilty sins of the world. Indeed, God foreknew the immediate need for man's redemption.

Step by step...we note the promises, the prophecies, and the symbolic meaning of the Old Testament types: to be fulfilled at God's appointed time. Indeed, they are all infallible, noting (Mat. 5:17-18). It is conceivable to note that from Genesis to Revelation "Christ is the theme of the Bible." Eternal love, mercy, and divine sovereignty have been revealed throughout the Inspired Word of God. The infallible foreknowledge of God is disclosed, noting the doctrine in the unique book of Genesis. The beginning of all things are clearly revealed. The advanced advent noting the promised Redeemer, "...the seed of the woman" is divinely emphasized; noting (Gen. 3:15, 12:3, 22:18, 49:10; noting Gal. 3:16). The special line and the race through whom the Messiah should come is disclosed.

Again, the Old Testament (animal) sacrificial types, shadows, and symbols were foreshadowed as a spiritual preparatory mean exemplified as substitutes, typified as the shadow of good things (Col. 2:17) to come. They were not realities (Heb. 10:3), but a preparatory mean that God's people could comprehend and become aware of the spiritual need for atonement from the guilt and the penalty of sin. The redemptive price, the ransom for sin, must be paid at God's appointed time.

God is love, and God is merciful. Looking back in Eden, visioning the first noted home of Adam and Eve, the coats of skins (Gen. 3:21) were garments divinely provided for Adam (v. 7) and the woman. It is not difficult to vision, conceiving it possible that an animal was slain, an indication of blood may have been visible.

Again, Abel's sacrifice (4:4-5; Heb. 11:4, 9:22) is noted, and approved by God as an excellent sacrifice. Abel's faith is noted. The shedding of blood parallels to Christ, the promised (Gen. 3:15) Redeemer, "The seed of the Woman."

The Almighty God is Infinite in every respect. God foreknew the source and the specified path, noting the destination by which His righteous seed (Gen. 3:15) would be sent forth (Gal. 4:4) into the world, noting the time and the place of the promised Redeemer's birth.

The Word (Logos) existed with God (John 1:1-2; 17:5) eternally, before all else. The Old Testament foreshadows the Messiah's coming in type, purposely positioned, symbolized, venerated, and authorized as the established agent-prophetically typified above all, according to the Will of God. "The fellowship of the mystery (Eph. 3:9) is noted."

Step by step, the designated path of the "seed" of the woman is unfoled (Gen. 3:15). It is a fact that "The purpose, and the plan of God can never, never be hindered." God's Word is infallible.

Looking back, visioning into the ancient past, noting the eternal purpose and plan of God, Abel was the second son of Adam (Gen. 4:1-9); his place was filled (v. 25) by Seth (the appointed one), the third son of Adam. Noah (6:8-10), was a descendant of Seth. Shem (9:26-27), one of Noah's three sons, the blessing (v. 23, 26) of Shem is unfold. The call (12:1-4) of Abraham is noted. Abraham was in the lineage of Shem. The promised son to Abraham (17:19-21) is unfold, "For in Isaac...shall thy seed by called...." Jacob (28:10-14); Judah (49:10). Here the Messianic prophecy is noted, "A star out of Jacob, from the tribe of Judah (Num. 24:17)." It is evident that our Lord sprang (Heb. 7:14) out of Judah, noting (Mat. 1:1). "The great God is the Supreme Being in all the earth, and in heaven." God knows the thoughts (Ps. 139:2) of man."

The dispensation of the promise is noted. The call (Gen. 12:1-3) came to Abram. The promises to Abram and his seed (v. 7) is revealed, "And in thee shall all families of the earth be blessed."" Our God is so merciful. God foresaw the dire need for the redemption of His people; aware that the payment of the price for sin...was a "costly sacrifice. "For all have sinned, and come short of the glory of God."

God chose Him a man, aware that he would be in total obedience; prayerful, and step by step, he would become a man of genuine faith. That man was Abraham (Gen. 22:1-18). Patriarch Abraham was one of God's great spiritual leaders. He was an earthly pattern as a guide to teach and enlighten the heathens, and generations to come that they might grasp and learn from the footsteps of Abraham, acquiring the zeal to live and walk in the righteousness of faith, noting (15:6). The covenant promises (15:18, 17:7) continued through the patriarchal line and race. The lineage of Abraham was divinely chosen as the specified lineage through whom the Messiah should come. The Abrahamic covenant was a by faith (Gal. 3:14-18) covenant, "that can not be disannulled." Step by step, God was working out history that He foresaw through Abraham. Sarah is also noted (Gen. 17:15-19). "By faith...Abraham looked for a city which hath foundations, whose builder and maker is God (Heb. 11:9-16)."

The book of Genesis narrates a sizeable history of the patriarchal age, and the leaders. The fellowship between man and God is noted.

The narrative story revealing the life history of Joseph discloseth much noting his steadfast faith, character, his forgiving spirit, his wisdom, and prudence. The descriptive traits portray Joseph's life as a man blessed with God-given wisdom, noting (Gen. 41:33).

The endeavors of Joseph as a lad (Gen. 37-50), and during his adult years in Egypt, God was with him. Joseph's life, and his deeds, point to the reality of faith, love, and hope for generations to come. He was a living light, an example for our youth today; "age is not limited."

Joseph's mind appeared to be centered, and wholly controlled by an indwelling divine agent very well known to Joseph. He was a lad, yet, he was a dreamer, an interpreter (Gen. 37:1-36; 41:1-37) of dreams. He was divinely blessed with the divination of prophecy. Pharaoh, and his servants immediately recognized the spirit of God (41:37-44) within Joseph who trusted in the God of Abraham, Isaac, and Jacob. God is the same yesterday, and today, and forever.

Joseph is credited (Gen. 39:,-41:,-42:) for saving the lives of the Hebrews (45:). The countries came into Egypt to Joseph to buy corn. The famine was sore over the earth, nevertheless, there was bread in Egypt. The Scripture (Ezek. 14:12-13) tells us one of the causes for the famine on the earth: "When the land sinneth against God."

During the famine, Joseph was reunited with his brethren who sold him (Gen. 37:23-28) into Egypt, noting (Ps. 105:16-21). He was falsely accused (Gen. 39:1-23) by Potiphar's wife, Joseph was put in prison. Joseph never appeared to be stressed, provoked, laden, nor did he ever appear to be indignant towards anyone. In the midst of Joseph's trials he always appeared to be Christ-like. Joseph refused to accept or welcome the opportunity to let the wiles of Satan disworth his being by harboring in his heart the pain and suffering from the piercing thorns of hate, which he willingly replaced with profound love. Joseph trusted in God to lead and guide his footsteps, remembering (50:24) the generations to come; Joseph expounded God's hand (45:7-8) in human events. The narrative account or story paralleling to Joseph's life, vividly proves himself as magnanimous, and indeed, trustworthy. He was a striking pattern for our youth to note and grasp today, Joseph was a radiant light for humankind to note "age is unlimited."

Looking back, reiterating the call (Gen. 12:1-3) and the promise to patriarch Abraham and his seed (v. 7), God foresaw the beginning of the nation Israel, through Abraham, who was the first patriarch and ancestor of the Hebrew race and nation. Through the foreknowledge of God, Abraham was aware that his descendants (the Israelites) would someday become afflicted (enslaved) in Egypt (15:13). The nation Israel were descendants of Abraham: "God's chosen family begin through patriarch Abraham, and Sarah." The Israelites were descendants of Israel (Jacob), began as a nation (Ex. 1:12; 20) in Egypt.

The unique book of Genesis unfolds the beginning of all creation (Gen. 1:1-2). Step by step, the accounts are noted. The book of Genesis ends with the prophecy (50:24-26) and the death of Joseph in Egypt. The descendants of Joseph and his brethren multiplied exceedingly in Egypt; they were under a new king who knew not Joseph. The foreknowledge (15:13-14) of God is noted as infallible, "In whom are hid all the treasures of wisdom and knowledge (Col. 2:3)."

The endeavors of Joseph provide historical background, unfolding sizable insight for the book of Exodus.

The Pentateuch contains the first five books of the Old Testament. The books (scrolls) are literally ascribed to the authorship of Moses.

Bondage inEgypt

The nation Israel were the descendants (Gen. 12:2) of patriarch Abraham, "Set apart (Ex. 19:6) as a holy nation." Through the family of Abraham (Gen. 12:3, 22:18, 49:10) and his wife Sarah (Gal. 3:16), a Savior would come to save the world, noting (Rom. 5:12-14). Isaac's birth (Gen. 17:16-19) was promised to Abraham and Sarah, noting (Heb. 11:18). The Abrahamic covenant (Gen.15:18) was an everlasting covenant. The maturing faith (12:13; 22:1-19) of Abraham is noted. The call of Abraham (12:1-4) was the beginning of God's chosen family, noting the promise (v. 3) of salvation.

The Israelites (35:9-12) were the descendants of Israel (Jacob) and began as a nation (Ex. 1:12; 20) in Egypt. Through the foreknowledge of God (Gen. 15:13-14), Israel's bondage was foreknown to patriarch Abraham (noting 15:6).

Indeed, the Bible is God's Inspired Word, "God's Word is infallible." The Bible has many books, nonetheless, the Bible is unfolding one story of God's everlasting love for His dear children. Redemption was God's plan. Salvation was purposed, and planned in eternity, before the foundation (Eph. 1:3-14) of the world. God reveals Himself in many ways to mankind, and through mankind.

Jacob (Israel) moved with his family to Egypt. There was seventy in number, Joseph was already (Gen. 46:) in Egypt. Jacob (Israel) was the father of the twelve tribes of Israel. The tribes were classified (Acts 7:8) as the twelve patriarchs, noting (v. 9).

Joseph died (Ex. 1:1-22), and all his brethren and all that generation. The children of Israel multiplied very rapidly, and the land was filled with them. The children of Israel were fruitful, and exceedingly mighty. They were now under a new king, and the taskmasters sought means to enslave the children of Israel by making life very bitter for them. "Pharaoh, and the Egyptians were very troubled because of the children of Israel."

God was in the foreknowledge of Israel's bondage in the land of Egypt. Indeed, God is wholly aware of our future, the days, the months, and the years of our lives.

Looking back, the narrative account relating to the life of Joseph (Gen. 37:-50:) in the land of Egypt unfolds as an enhancing example for both our youth and adults. He was sold into slavery by his own brethren, nonetheless, he proved himself to be divinely motivated. Joseph was kindhearted, forgiving with profound concern. He was trustworthy and faithful in all of his endeavors (45.17-28).

The narrative account of Joseph's life supplies great insight, unfolding and providing historical background for the doctrine of the book of Exodus. The book of Exodus supplies Israel's history, unfolding God's redemptive plan to redeem a slave nation out of bondage in Egypt. The book of Exodus denotes departure, the liberation of God's chosen people at His appointed time.

The new king and the Egyptians sought means to enslave the children of Israel, that they might control and execute cruel treatment upon them. Indeed, the orders that were commanded (Ex. 1:7-22) by Pharaoh to bring affliction upon the children of Israel were very inhuman. The bodily strength or physical power within the nation Israel was constantly multiplying. The new king was troubled. He assumed the children of Israel might join other enemies in war and fight against them. The king carefully observed the mightiness of the nation Israel. The future for the children of Israel faced indefinite misery, noting the ill will and the demands requested by the taskmasters, who were very oppressive.

The God of Abraham, Isaac, and Jacob was concerned about the condition of the children of Israel, a slave nation in bondage without a leader to liberate them. It is possible, periodically during the Israelites' affliction, that they wondered if God would fail them, forgetting that the promises of God are infallible.

The Scripture (Ex. 2:1-10) tells us a goodly child was born in Egypt, the son of Amram and Jochebed, the brother of Aaron and Miriam. The child was born under slavery. The mother was aware that Pharaoh sought death for all male Hebrew newborns. Indeed, God is love, and God is merciful. The mother Jochebed concluded she could no longer hide the child from harm's way. She then sought means to save her child from the edict of death.

The mother was blessed with divine wisdom, that only the Almighty God can impart. Jochebed created a basket-like waterproof ark. It is conceivable to believe, by means, the mother was certain in mind, that the basket she had created was completely secured from leakage and adequately lined for the Child's contentment. The mother placed the child in the basket. Carefully carrying her precious child, she made her way down to the brink of the river. She securely closed and fastened the lid, the covering for the little ark. The mother put the ark among the flags in the shallow water, close to the river's brink.

It is possible the mother of the child was not aware that Miriam, the child's sister, had followed her down to the river quietly remaining out of the sight of her mother. Nonetheless, Miriam purposely remained within eye view of the basket-like ark that sheltered this godly child.

The mother Jochebed recognized the child was comely, unaware that the child she hid from the edict of death commanded by Pharaoh would become God's chosen one, at His appointed time. "God's redemptive plans are infallible."

Miriam was constantly watching the ark when she saw strangers nearing the brink of the river. The daughter of Pharaoh came down to the river to bathe, her maidens were walking along by the river's side. She saw the ark in the shallow water amid the flags and sent her maid to bring the ark. When she opened it, she saw the child, and behold, the babe wept. And she had compassion on him and said, "This is one of the Hebrews' children (vs. 6-8)." Then said his sister to Pharaoh's daughter, "Shall I go and call thee a nurse of the Hebrew women, that she may nurse the child for thee?" And Pharaoh's daughter said to her, "Go." And the maid went and called the child's mother. Pharaoh's daughter paid the child's mother wages to care for the child until he become of age to join the royal palace.

It is conceivable to believe that because of Pharaoh's daughter's concern for the child's future knowledge, she deemed it wise and very important that the child should be wholly aware of his family history. It is possible the mother of the child was instructed by Pharaoh's daughter to relate to the child the history of the forefathers, noting patriarch Abraham, Isaac, and Jacob (Israel), noting the courageous life of

Joseph in Egypt, the Israelite history of his parents, and the fact that he was born under slavery, under the edict of death.

Pharaoh's daughter adopted the child as her son. She named the child Moses, who was left in the care of his mother until he was old enough to live in the royal palace, within royal surroundings. "If God be for us...who can be against us....?" "For the Lord of hosts hath purposed...and who shall disannul it....?"

Moses was educated in all the wisdom of the Egyptians. He was mighty in words, and in deeds. "By faith Moses, when he was come to years; refused to be called the son of Pharaoh's daughter," noting (Heb. 11:24). Moses was profoundly concerned about the well-being of his people: He was wholly aware that the new king (Pharaoh) had enslaved his people, the Hebrews. The Scripture (Acts 7:23) tells us, "And when he was full forty years old, it came into his heart to visit his brethren, the children of Israel."

It is conceivable to believe that Moses was aware of the burdens of his people. "Moses identifies himself with Israel." It was his choice to leave the royal court, "choosing rather to suffer affliction with the people of God, than to enjoy the pleasures of sin for a second." (Heb. 11:25).

Moses spent the first forty years of his life in the surroundings of the royal court, until he felt the need to mingle with his brethren. During Moses' association with his people, he observed an Egyptian striking an Hebrew, one of his brethren, with great force. It is possible a violent rage came over Moses. He slew the Egyptian, covered him with sand, and left Egypt (Ex. 2:11-15) because he feared for his life. Moses fled, and dwelt in the land of Midian (vs. 16-22), where he met the priest of Midian. The priest gave Moses one of his seven daughters, her name was Zipporah. "And she bare him a son...his name was Gershom." And the name of the other son (18:4) was Eliezer, "for the God of my father," said he, "was mine help, and delivered me from the sword of Pharaoh."

Indeed, Jacob and his descendants (Gen. 46:-47:) were once warmly welcome to dwell in Egypt, in the rich land of Goshen. Under the late ruler Pharaoh, Joseph is also noted. In the process of time, the new king Pharaoh of Egypt died. The welfare pertaining to the children of Israel declined into less favorable circumstances. The children of Israel sighed, expressing profound sorrow; by reason of the bondage they cried. Their suffering was a painful experience. God was wholly aware (Gen. 15:13-18) of Israel's afflection. The fore knowledge of God is infallible.

God was concerned about the immediate condition, and the future of the new nation Israel. God heard the groaning (Ex. 2:24-25) of the children of Israel and remembered His covenant with Abraham, Isaac, and Jacob, and God has special esteem for the children of Israel. The deliverance of Israel was very essential. God had a purpose and plan for the nation Israel, and God acted through His divine operation to deliver them from bondage in Egypt. Redemption is wholly of God.

Jethro was the priest of Midian and the father-in-law of Moses, who was the shepherd of Jethro's flock. It is possible Moses led the flock to the backside of the desert daily, and came to the mountain of God, even to Horeb.

In ancient times, shepherds equipped themselves with certain necessities such as a rod (a stick) used for support or as a protective weapon. Moses spent forty years in the desert.

It is conceivable to believe that while the flock grazed, Moses observed the divine handi-work surrounding Horeb, the mountain of God. It is also possible that Moses periodically reclined, looking skyward, noting the beautiful azure sky, his mind often retracing back to the welfare of his brethren in Egypt, under the oppression of the taskmasters.

It is possible that Moses, treading to and from the backside of the mountain of God, observed nature in its entirety and beauty; silently unfolding a visible message, a divine testimony, "Only God could have placed them there."

And the angel of the Lord appeared unto him in a flame of fire out of the midst of a bush. And he looked, and behold, the bush burned with fire, and the bush was not consumed (Ex. 3:). "God called unto Moses...out of the midst of the bush, and said, Moses, Moses. And he said, Here am I...." And He said, "Draw not nigh hither: put off thy shoes from off thy feet, for the place whereon thou standest is holy ground." And the Lord said, I have surely seen the affliction of my people which are in Egypt, and I have heard their cry by reason of their taskmasters; for I know their sorrows, "And I am come down to deliver them...out of the hand of the Egyptians, and to bring them up out of that land unto a good land and a large, unto a land flowing with milk and honey...."

God identified Himself (v. 6) to Moses, "Saying, I am the God of thy father, the God of Abraham, the God of Isaac, and the God of Jacob...." Moses heard the same voice that called (Gen. 3:9) unto Adam in the garden of Eden. Moses hid his face, for he was afraid to look upon God.

God was wholly aware and concerned about the Egyptians oppressing His people. God commissioned Moses to deliver Israel out of bondage in Egypt. "Come now therefore, and I will send thee unto Pharaoh, that thou mayest bring forth my people the children of Israel out of Egypt (Ex. 3:10-22)."

"And Moses said unto God: Who am I, that I should go unto Pharaoh, and that I should bring forth the children of Israel out of Egypt?"

It is possible Moses pondered for a moment, and visioned himself in confrontation with Pharaoh, who was a very stubborn king, rebellious, and debasing. Also the task as that of a father, the liberation of the children of Israel out of bondage in Egypt. Divine assurance rids the mind of weakness, fears, and doubts.

It is also possible Moses felt he did not have the strength, nor the power, to accomplish Israel's deliverance alone, not realizing that God is sovereign, able to prepare His chosen with every need to accomplish His divine will. At God's appointed time, Moses was sure to acquire the utmost certainty, trusting in himself, and trusting in the promises of God (vs. 12-22). God promised Moses He would be with him. "When thou hast brought forth the people out of Egypt...ye shall serve God upon this mountain."

And Moses said unto God, "Behold, when I come unto the children of Israel, and shall say unto them: The God of your fathers hath sent me unto you; and they shall say to me, What is His name? What shall I say unto them?" "And God said unto Moses, ... I AM THAT I AM: and He said, Thus shalt thou say unto the children of Israel, I AM hath sent me unto you." Indeed, there is utmost (all) power in the name of I AM the Almighty God; His wonders (v. 20) will unfold.

Moses complained (Ex. 4:1-17), argued with God, making known his inadequateness, his unworthiness, his lack of abilities to undertake a task so great. Moses expressed his humble opinion about himself unto the Lord.

"Moses complained...that the children of Israel will not believe me, nor hearken unto my voice: for they will say: The Lord hath not appeared unto thee...."

And the Lord said unto him, "What is that in thine hand? And he said, A rod. And He said: Cast it on the ground, and it became a serpent; and Moses fled from before it. And it shall come to pass, if they will not believe thee, neither hearken to the voice of the first sign, that they will believe the voice of the latter sign."

And Moses said unto the Lord, "O my Lord, I am not eloquent, neither heretofore, nor since Thou hast spoken unto Thy servant: but I am slow of speech, and of a slow tongue. The Lord (v. 11) questioned Moses: And the Lord said unto him, Who hath made man's mouth?

"Now therefore go, and I will be with thy mouth, and teach thee what thou shalt say."

It appears Moses profoundly sensed the fact that he was incapable of liberating the children of Israel out of bondage in Egypt. "And he said, O my Lord, send, I pray thee, by the hand of him whom Thou wilt send." Moses sensed the fact that without the name, and the power, and the divine message of authority be given unto him from God, to be related unto the children of Israel, his own conjurement unto Israel without divine power would have been in vain.

It is conceivable to believe that Moses pondered before complaining unto God, and concluded that the responsibility was far too great for him to engage in alone. Moses desired not to rely upon himself, but to rely upon God for Israel's redemption or deliverance. God made Himself known unto Moses (Ex. 3:2, 12) out of the midst of the burning bush, and God promised Moses that He would be with him. Still, Moses complained and objected unto the Lord, requesting (4:13) some other person in his stead. "And the anger of the Lord was kindled against Moses,...and He said: Is not Aaron the Le'vite thy brother? I know he can speak well...." And he shall be the spokesman unto the people (vs. 14-17): "And thou shalt take this rod in thine hand, wherewith thou shalt do signs." Israel's deliverance was certain, by divine power. Moses' hand was divinely prepared to hold and activate the rod of God, the sign of authority.

In due time, Moses would surmount, realizing the realness of the power, and the promises (Ex. 3:11-15) of God. It is a fact that when man yields to the call, and to the will of God, all obstacles fail to become a hindrance. The God of Abraham calls His chosen out of the world, and commissions them for service (mission). God empowers, and God anoints by His Spirit, instilling Himself within His chosen. God is able to impart His Spirit, and His power within His chosen ones, before sending them out into the world. If we are willing, God is able to prepare us for any given task.

Step by step, the manifestation of God's divine presence and His divine power is certain to unfold. Pharaoh, all the kings, and all nations, will recognize the fact that God's purpose and God's plans are unfailing. Indeed, the children of Israel were under the command and the control of the new king Pharaoh. Nonetheless, the children of Israel were always under the divine power and the surveillance of the Almighty God. Israel was an enslaved nation-a multitude through whom the Messiah would come.

Redemption was God's plan. God is working, operating by His divine power, through the activation of Moses, and his miracle rod, the rod of authority, to liberate the children of Israel out of bondage in Egypt.

Divinely anointed, Moses was willing to accept, and obey the voice of the Lord (Ex. 4:15-18). Moses was wholly cognizant, he held in his hand divine power within his miracle rod, "The rod of God." Moses was anticipating his mission of deliverance (vs. 19-31), (Heb. 11:27-29) by, and with steadfast faith in, the Almighty God. His miraculous works (signs, and wonders) are all infallible.

It is not noted that Moses was seeking God favorably. God foresaw Israel's deliverance through the call and the commission of Moses, who observed the divine miraculous wonders of the Lord and the signs that he was able to perform with his rod, through divine power. Moses' trust in the promises of God, became a reality.

Moses returned to Jethro, his father-in-law, with a requisite, a verbal request, desiring to return (4:18-26) unto his brethren in Egypt, unaware if they were still alive. Moses was wholly aware of the Egyptian people and their culture. Moses was also aware that his people were in the immediate need of a leader to liberate them out of bondage of Egypt. Jethro told Moses to go in peace.

And the Lord said unto Moses in Midian, go, return into Egypt, for all the men are dead which sought thy life. "And thou shalt take this rod in thine hand, wherewith thou shalt do signs." Moses and his family returned to the land of Egypt and Moses took the rod of God in his hand. The Lord sent Aaron into the wilderness to meet Moses, in the mount of God (vs. 14-16; 19-27).

And Moses and Aaron went and gathered together all the elders of the children of Israel. And Aaron spake all the words which the Lord had spoken unto Moses, and did the signs in the sight of the people. "And the people believed: and when they heard that the Lord had visited the children of Israel...and that He had looked upon their affliction...then they bowed their heads and worshipped.

Moses and Aaron went in to Pharaoh with the first demand from the Lord of Israel, "Let my people go, that they may hold a feast unto Me in the wilderness." And Pharaoh said, "Who is the Lord, that I should obey His voice...to let Israel go? I know not the Lord, neither will I let Israel go." Moses and Aaron related the second demand of God to Pharaoh. Again, Pharaoh's heart hardened. The demand was a three day journey into the desert, that they might sacrifice unto the Lord their God, lest He fall upon us with pestilence, or with the sword (harmful or dangerous). It would have been impossible for the nation Israel to sacrifice or serve the Lord their God in Egypt (Ex. 8:26-32), because some animals, such as bulls and cows, were noted as very sacred within the practices of the Egyptians.

The burdens of Israel increased. The officers of the Israelites were beaten by the taskmasters because they were not given the needed supplies (Ex. 5:) to fulfill the task of making brick. The officers complained to Moses and Aaron, "And Moses returned unto the Lord, and said: Lord, wherefore hast Thou so evil entreated this people? Why is it that Thou hast sent me? For since I came to Pharaoh to speak in Thy name, he hath done evil to this people; neither hast Thou delivered Thy people at all. Then the Lord said unto Moses: Now shalt thou see what I will do to Pharaoh."

Both Moses and Aaron were commanded (Ex. 6:13) to bring the children of Israel out of the land of Egypt. "I will harden Pharaoh's heart, and multiply my signs and wonders in the land of Egypt: And the Egyptians shall know (Ex. 7:) that I am the Lord. When I stretch forth mine hand upon Egypt, and bring out the children of Israel from among them."

The miracles and the plagues were made possible by the divine power, and the miracle rod of God. The demands of God upon Pharaoh were made known to him by and through Moses. Still, Pharaoh refused to yield unto the Lord. The miracles of the Lord will be observed and recognized by Pharaoh and his servants. The Israelites will not be affected by any of the plagues. There were ten plagues activated by the power of the Lord, through Moses and Aaron (noting Ex. 12:). The severeness of the tenth (last) plague influenced Pharaoh to let Moses fulfill the task of leading the children of Israel out of bondage in Egypt.

The first plague is noted, "and the Lord spake unto Moses: Say unto Aaron, Take thy rod, and stretch out thine hand upon the waters of Egypt, upon their streams, upon their rivers, and upon their ponds, and upon all their pools of water, that they may become blood: and that there may be blood throughout the land of Egypt, both in vessels of wood, and in vessels of stone." The waters of Egypt (Ex. 7:19-21) land turned to blood. The second plague, the frogs came up, and covered the land of Egypt. The third plague, the dust of the earth, became lice...throughout all the land of Egypt. The fourth plague, the land of Egypt was corrupted by reason of the swarm of flies. The fifth plague, all the cattle in Egypt died. The sixth plague, the ashes that the Lord told Moses to sprinkle towards the heavens became dust throughout Egypt, causing boils and blains upon man and beast. The seventh plague, the Lord rained hail upon the land of Egypt. The eighth plague the locusts covered the face of the whole earth, so that the land was darkened. The ninth plague, The land of Egypt was dark for three days. "And the Lord said unto Moses: Yet will I bring one plague more upon Pharaoh, and upon Egypt; afterwards he will let you go hence: When he shall let you go, he shall surely thrust you out hence altogether. And Moses said, Thus saith the Lord, "About midnight will I go out into the midst of Egypt:" And all the firstborn of man, and beast shall die in the land of Egypt. And the Lord gave the people favor in the sight of the Egyptians (Ex. 11:1-7)." In due time, Pharaoh and his servants would come to bow down unto the Lord.

Pharaoh's heart was hardened by the Lord, so that he would not let the children of Israel go out of the land. He refused to submit to the demands (Ex. 11:8-10) of the Lord. Both Pharaoh and his servants would come to recognize the fact that Pharaoh's power was earthly and limited, but the power of the Lord is heavenly, and is unlimited. The power of the Lord was recognized and acknowledged by the Magicians (8:) "This is the finger of God."

The Lord promised to redeem Israel with a stretched out arm, and with great judgments (Ex. 6:6-8). The tenth judgment, the last plague will bring about Israel's deliverance from bondage in Egypt. The death of the firstborn, will cause a great cry throughout Egypt and Pharaoh will hastily thrust Israel out of the land.

The passover was instituted. The passover is commemorative of the tenth plague (Ex. 12:1-28). The passover, a Jewish festival, commemorates the exodus from Egypt.

The preparation for the passover is noted. The lamb, a male of the first year, shall be without blemish, noting (I Pet. 1:19). The lamb must be slain in the evening. And they shall take of the blood, and strike it on the two side posts and on the upper door post of the houses, wherein they shall eat it. "The blood of the lamb must be applied (Ex. 12:12-14)." When I see the blood, I will pass over you. The manifestation of the blood, spiritually perceived (vs. 7; 22-28) as a type. "Only the applied blood of the lamb could secure, save the children of Israel from the great judgment, "the Death Angel." The applied blood sprinkled at the door was a sign of obedience to God, in faith. The blood was a token, that rendered or gave hope and peace within the houses of the Hebrews. They believed (v. 12) in the divine promise (v. 23) of the Lord.

"And it came to pass, that at midnight the Lord smote all the firstborn in the land of Egypt, from the firstborn of Pharaoh that sat on his throne unto the firstborn of the captive that was in the dungeon; and all the firstborn of the cattle...There was a great cry in Egypt: for there was not a house where there was not one dead."

The promises of the Lord are unfailing (Rom. 9:4). The Israelites were God's chosen people. They were identified (Gen. 3:15; 12:1-3; 49:10; Rom. 9:4-13, Ex. 14:13) in God's divine plan of salvation.

The Lord gave His people special favor in the sight of the Egyptians. Indeed, the rod of Moses was the sign of (Ex. 4:17, 20) divine authority. The firstborn of the Lord was redeemed, secured by the blood of the lamb (12:11-14) (Ex. 13:2).

The Exodus

Adventure in the Wilderness

God promised (Ex. 6:6-7) to redeem Israel, liberating them with a stretched out arm, and with great judgement. God heard the groaning (2:24) of the children of Israel, and God remembered His covenant with Abraham, Isaac, and Jacob. Indeed, the promises of God will never fail (infallible).

The intervening of the Death Angel's work at midnight (Ex. 12:29-42) persuaded Pharaoh the king to thrust Israel out of the land of Egypt in haste.

God's people (Israel) were prepared, ready to leave out of Egypt (v. 34). In haste they journeyed from Rameses to Succoth, about six hundred thousand on foot that were men, beside children. And a mixed multitude went up also with them (vs. 38-39), they were thrust out of Egypt, and could not tarry, neither had they prepared for themselves any victual. "Indeed, God is man's Creator, wholly in the foreknowledge of man's every need, and God will provide." God gave His divine assurance to Israel, that they might acquire the utmost certainty (Ex. 11:7), that the Lord God would bring Israel safely into the land of promise (Heb. 11:9).

Now the sojourning (Ex. 12:40-51) of the children of Israel who dwelt in Egypt, was four hundred and thirty years. It is a night to be much observed unto the Lord for bringing them out from the land of Egypt. This is the night of the Lord to be observed of all the children of Israel in their generations. The ordinance of the passover (vs. 43-51) is noted.

The Sanctification (Ex. 13:) of the firstborn unto God is observed. The law of the feast of unleavened bread, and the law relating to the firstborn is noted.

The children of Israel were divinely led about, through the way of the wilderness of the Red Sea. The Scripture (vs. 17-18) tells us that the children of Israel went up out of the land of Egypt harnessed, they were equipped for a wilderness adventure that was unknown to them.

Joseph's request (Gen. 50:24-25) was fulfilled, before the nation Israel left Egypt. Moses took the bones of Joseph with him, during the early morning of the exodus.

Indeed, Pharaoh and his servants (Ex. 11:8; 12:31-34) did yield hastily unto the voice of the Lord, and bowed themselves unto the Lord. Indeed, man must realize who God is: God is the Creator, the maker, and the ruler of the whole universe. God is infallible, God is the same yesterday, and today, and forever. "The miraculous acts of God reveal His divine power to all mankind." "For He knoweth our frame; He remembereth that we (Ps. 103:14) are dust." God is the Rock (Deut. 32:4), His work is perfect. God's work is everlasting.

Under God's command, Moses led the children of Israel, about six hundred thousand on foot, through the way of the wilderness of the Red Sea. They encamped in Etham, on the edge of the wilderness. The journey (Num. 33:) is noted. Moses believed the promises of God; he was satisfied that the God of Abraham, Isaac, Jacob, and Joseph would always be with him (Ex. 3:12-14), supplying him with the needed strength and wisdom to fulfill the task that he was chosen to perform. They were redeemed with a stretched out arm (6:6-7), and with great judgment. The God of all creation was/is the Supreme Engineer, the Source of all power.

During the commencing of the journey, and throughout the exodus, the divine presence of the Lord was always visible for the host of Israelites to observe, and believe that the God of Abraham was with them. God was the guiding light for the children of Israel (Ex. 13:21-22), from Egypt to Canaan.

The Lord went before them by day in a pillar of a cloud, to lead them the way; and by night in a pillar of fire, to give them light, to go by day and night. The Lord was wholly directing the exodus journey, through the leadership of Moses, who was God's chosen leader for the task.

God, who is in the foreknowledge of all things, knew the thoughts of Pharaoh, "For Pharaoh will say of the children of Israel: They are entangled in the land, the wilderness hath shut them in." Nonetheless, if God be for us, who can be against us? The Lord hardened Pharaoh's heart (Ex. 14:3-31), that Pharaoh and his host might follow them, and they did so. Under the divine surveillance of the Lord, the children of Israel had gone out of Egypt, in the early morning hours, with a high hand.

Pharaoh, the king of Egypt, his horsemen, and his army, pursued after the children of Israel and overtook them while they were encamping by the sea. It is possible, while the children of Israel were journeying through the desert regions in the wilderness, their spirits were low because of the intense heat rays from the sun and the breeze that chilled their bodies in the night...and now the thought of the cruel Egyptians pursuing after them?

It is conceivable to believe that the Israelites periodically observed the large body of water, the Red Sea, and had questions in the back of their minds...How were they going to cross the sea or were the Egyptians avertible? The Egyptians' horsemen, six hundred chosen chariots, and all the chariots of Egypt were drawing nearer and nearer to the sea, where the Israelites were encamped.

The children of Israel lifted up their eyes, aware that the Egyptians were marching after them. They were terrified. It is conceivable to believe the children of Israel did not quite forget the blessings of the Lord, nor the promises of the God of Abraham, Isaac, Jacob, and Joseph. But due to their immediate circumstances, they seemed not to quite recall the Lord's promises, nor His presence (Ex. 6:6-7; 12:41-42; 13:21-22), noting that the Lord had redeemed them from bondage, with a stretched out arm, and with great judgment. Nonetheless, they cried out (v. 10) unto the Lord, and complained unto Moses (14:11-12) with a question, "Hast thou taken us away...to die in the wilderness....?"

"And Moses said unto the people, Fear ye not, stand still, and see the salvation of the Lord, which He will show you today. For the Egyptians whom ye have seen today, ye shall see them again no more for ever." The Lord shall fight for you, and ye shall hold your peace.

The Lord commanded Moses to speak unto the children of Israel, that they go forward. "But lift up thy rod, and stretch out thine hand over the sea, and divide it: and the children of Israel shall go on dry ground through the midst of the sea." The Lord hardened the hearts of the Egyptians, that they might follow the children of

Israel. And the Lord was certain to receive honor from Pharaoh, and upon his host, upon his chariots, and upon his horsemen. "I am the Lord." Pharaoh's power was earthly and limited, but the power of the Lord is unlimited, and is eternal.

The Scriptures tell us the angel of God, which went before the camp of Israel, removed and went behind them; and the pillar of the cloud went from before their face, and stood behind them. And it came between the camp of the Egyptians, and the camp of Israel; and it was a cloud and darkness to them, but it gave light by night to these so that the one came not near the other (Ex. 14:13-31) all the night. "What shall we then say to these things? If God be for us, who can be against us?"

The Egyptians were marching within close range in the sight of the frightened Israelites. It is conceivable to believe the chariots and the heavily armoured Pharaoh, and his horsemen were in eye-sight of the Israelites; but the God of Abraham, Isaac, and Jacob was there, in the midst of His people, to save them from the Egyptians. Let us note again, the divine power of God, unfolding, and activated (vs. 21-31) through Moses and his rod of divine authority. Moses had steadfast faith in God and His divine power. All the miraculous acts of God are factual and unsearchable.

Moses was obedient to God's command. Moses stretched out his hand (trusting in God) towards the waters of the Red Sea. The Scriptures tell us the Lord caused the sea to go back by a strong east wind all night, and made the sea dry land, and the waters were divided (congealed v. 8). And the children of Israel went into the midst of the sea upon dry ground and the waters were a wall unto them on their right hand, and on their left. "The Egyptians pursued, and went in after them to the midst of the sea (vs. 23-25)...." "The Lord troubled the host of the Egyptians...." The chariot wheels were taken of by divine authority, that they drave them heavily. The Egyptians were aware that God was fighting for Israel, His people. "The Lord commanded Moses to stretch his hand over the sea, that the waters may come again upon the Egyptians, upon their chariots, and upon their horsemen." Through the divine power of the Lord, Moses stretched forth his hand over the sea, and the sea returned to his strength. "The Lord saved Israel that day out of the hand of the Egyptians" and Israel saw the Egyptians dead upon the sea shore. "Israel saw the great work of the Lord, and the people feared the Lord, and believed the Lord, and His servant Moses." God promised (Ex. 6:5-8) Israel's redemption. They were redeemed by the mighty hand of God. The divine act, the miracle of God was made possible, that the children of Israel were able to stand on the other side of the Red Sea, observing the enemies, as they were destroyed by the miraculous power of God, noting (Deut. 26:6-8). Having observed the Red Sea miracle, the children of Israel were left with little or no doubt that all things are possible with the Lord God, and they feared the Lord, and believed the Lord, and His servant Moses. With man, the divine acts, the wonders, the miracles, and the signs were made possible, to be activated by Moses and Aaron, through the divine power of the Lord our God. "To whom then will ye liken God?" (Is. 40:17-18; Deut. 11:1-4). "With men this is impossible; but with God all things are possible."

After crossing the Red Sea, the first song of Israel is noted. Then sang Moses and the children of Israel, this song unto the Lord, and spake, saying, "I will sing unto the Lord, for He hath triumphed gloriously: the horse and his rider hath He thrown into the sea. The Lord is my strength, and song, and He has become my salvation: Thy right hand, O Lord, has become glorious in power: Thy right hand O Lord, hath dashed in pieces the enemies. The Lord shall reign forever and ever." And Miriam, the prophetess, the sister of Aaron, took a timbrel in her hand, and all the women went out after her with timbrels and with dances.

Moses and the children of Israel started on their journey from the Red Sea to Marah. Moses brought the children of Israel from the Red Sea, and they went into the wilderness of Shur. They went three days in the wilderness and found no water. They came to the waters of Marah. It is very possible when the children of Israel saw the waters of Marah, they immediately assumed their desire or craving for water was over, and their distressful thirst had come to an end. They were not aware that the waters of Marah were bitter; unfit for humankind, also animals. It is conceivable to believe the Israelites were very weary from their wilderness journey to the waters of Marah, and the people were overcome with strong emotions; they murmured against Moses. It is a fact that God hears, sees, and ponders the hearts of all (Mat. 12:36-37) humankind.

The people complained against their leader, nonetheless, Moses was a praying man. He cried unto the Lord, and the Lord shewed Moses a tree, which when he had cast into the waters, the waters were made sweet (Ex. 15:22-25). The healing covenant (v. 26) is noted, with conditions.

The wilderness journey continued (Ex. 16:) from Marah to Elim, into the wilderness of Sin. Israel was between Elim and Sinai. The whole congregation of the children of Israel murmured against Moses and Aaron. Periodically, their minds recollected back in the land of Egypt (v. 3) "Would to God we had died by the hand of the Lord in the land of Egypt, when we sat by the flesh pots, and when we did eat bread to the full; for ye have brought us forth into this wilderness, to kill this whole assembly with hunger."

The divine testing of the children of Israel is noted. Step by step, Israel was proved by the Lord thy God, whether they would obey, and walk in God's law.

Through Moses, God promised bread from heaven. Moses and Aaron said unto all the children of Israel, "At even, then ye shall know that the Lord hath brought you out from the land of Egypt." Moses related to the children of Israel that the Lord heareth your murmurings, which ye murmur against Him. "And behold, the glory of the Lord appeared in the cloud, unto the whole congregation...." "The Lord promised quails, and manna." "At even, ye shall eat flesh, and in the morning ye shall be filled with bread; and ye shall know that I am the Lord your God." God was aware of Israel's unbelief, and many divine miracles were emphasized. And it came to pass that at even the quails came up and covered the camp. And in the morning, the dew lay round about the host. "And when the children of Israel saw it, they said one to another: It is manna: for they wist not what it was." "And Moses said unto them: This is the bread which the Lord hath given you to eat." God promised Moses (v. 4) that He would rain bread from heaven for him, that the people might be filled with bread. The Lord commanded the law of manna, (vs. 16-35).

According to the commandments of the Lord, the children of Israel journeyed from the wilderness of Sin to the Rephidim plains, which was a camping site in the wilderness before they reached Sinai. The children of Israel were very thirsty, after wondering over the sandy desert region, still, the children of Israel proved themselves to be unbelieving, stubborn, and rebellious. They had observed many miraculous acts of God activated by and through Moses, demonstrating the divine power within his rod, "the rod of God."

The children of Israel were not brought out of Egypt to die of thirst; many miracles were performed to prove Israel, to see if they would obey God. The Lord commanded Moses to go before the people and take of the elders of Israel, and thy rod, wherewith thou smotest the river, take in thine hand and go. "Behold. I stand before thee there upon the rock in Horeb; and thou shalt smite the rock, and there shall come water out of it, that the people may drink...."

Because of Israel's murmuring, they tempted the Lord, saying, "Is the Lord among us, or not?" (Ex. 17:1-7). The Lord was aware of Israel's unbelieving hearts, nonetheless, the Lord provided for the children of Israel. They ate manna forty years, until they came unto the borders of the land of Canaan. The Lord commanded an omer of manna to be kept for future (16:) generations, that they may see the bread wherewith I fed you in the wilderness, when I brought you forth from the land of Egypt.

God delivered Israel out of bondage in Egypt. With a stretched-out arm they were led by the way of the Red Sea. The Lord led them through the wilderness by day in a pillar of a cloud, to lead them the way; and by night in a pillar of fire, to give them light, to go by day and night. The Lord made the bitter water sweet (Ex. 15:22-25), that their thirst might be quenched. The Lord promised and provided bread from heaven, and at even they had flesh to eat, the quails covered the camp. Israel (Num. 11:4-6) still complained.

The battle of Rephidim is noted. Amalek fought with Israel in Rephidim (Ex. 17:8-16). The divine miracle of the Lord unfolded in battle. Moses trusted in the God of the patriarchs, Abraham, Isaac, and Jacob, to victoriously fight Israel's battle (Ex. 17:8-16) with the rod of God.

The Lord performed many great miracles to prove to the children of Israel, also to prove to the people that the Lord was always in their midst, providing for them. God loved and redeemed his people. God had a purpose and plan for future generations through the nation Israel. The Lord was wholly aware of the thoughts of the children of Israel (Num. 14:1-35; Jude 5), nonetheless, the Lord continued to perform great miracles, aware of Israel's unbelief.

Moses was reunited with his family (Ex. 18:1-27) in the plain of Rephidim, a camping site of the Hebrews in the wilderness before they reached the Sinai desert. And Jethro, Moses' father-in-law, came with his sons and his wife unto Moses into the wilderness, where he encamped at the mount of God. Moses told his father-in-law about the miracles of God, how the Lord delivered them. "And Jethro said: Now I know the Lord is greater than all gods: for in the thing wherein they dealt proudly He was above them." Jethro took a burnt offering and sacrificed for God.

Jethro noted that Moses sat in long court sessions from the morning unto the evening, instructing the people. They stood in the midst of Moses from the morning unto the close of the day enquiring of God. Moses related to the people the statutes of God, and His laws.

Jethro was concerned about the wearing away of both Moses and the people. "Hearken now unto my voice, I will give thee counsel, and God shall be with thee...." Jethro advised Moses to seek divine command, get the will of God (v. 23) in all of his plans, and all will be well for both him and for his people, noting (Ex. 18:1-27; noting v. 25). Moses obeyed the advice of Jethro, his father-in-law. And Moses let his father-in-law depart; and he went his way into his own land. Moses spent forty years

(Ex. 2:15-21) in Midian. "The call of Moses (Ex. 3:) and the burning bush" is noted. "The flame was maintained by divine power."

Moses led the people from Rephidim to Sinai. For they were departed for Rephidim, and were come to the desert of Sinai, and had pitched in the wilderness; and there Israel camped before the mount, noting (Ex. 19:). "When thou hast brought forth the people out of Egypt, ye shall serve God upon this mountain...." God's promises are infallible. Israel arrived at Mt. Sinai, where Moses was to receive the law. Indeed, Moses demonstrated his life as a devoted servant of God, in all his dealings. Moses was faithful to God, and he was faithful to his people throughout the journey. Moses led his people with an unselfish heart that was full of profound love for God, and his people.

From generation to generation, Israel's deliverance from bondage down in Egypt was to be kept as a memorial by the children of Israel as a commemorative feast to the Lord. The great miracles of the Lord God is noted (Ex. 6:6-7, 12:1-28). Israel came up out of Egypt by the power of the stretched-out arm of the Lord. Indeed, God had a purpose and plan for the future of the children of Israel, through the leadership of Moses. "The burning bush is noted."

During the wilderness journey, the children of Israel were sometimes dismayed because of unbelief. There were times the children of Israel were disobedient, and rebellious unto God and Moses. Nonetheless, both God and Moses were concerned about the children of Israel. Moses prayed to God for the sins of the children of Israel. Moses steadfastly trusted in the God of Abraham for ample strength and sufficient wisdom to lead the children of Israel out of bondage in Egypt.

The children of Israel had observed the plagues, the wonders, and many divine miracles as they journeyed throughout the wilderness. The wilderness journey led the children of Israel from down in Egypt to the Red Sea, under the leadership of Moses. Through the power of the Lord (Ex. 14:13-31), the children of Israel crossed the Red Sea on dry land. The Scripture (13:21) tells us, "And the Lord went before them by day in a pillar of a cloud, to lead them the way; and by night in a pillar of fire, to give them light; to go by day and night." Redemption is wholly of God. Redemption is by blood (12:7-14, 1 Pet. 1:19); redemption is by power (Ex. 6:6; 13; 14), (Ps. 66:7). The Passover (Ex. 12:25-28) is noted, to be preserved forever, in the commemoration of the exodus from Egypt. The sacrificial animal's blood must be (v. 7) applied, noting (I Pet. 1:18-19). Israel was perfectly protected from the Death Angel (Ex. 12:12-13) through the power of the Lord. Redemption is wholly of God.

The children of Israel had many encampments during the wilderness journey; many times they were faced with situations, they murmured (Ex. 16:7) against the Lord; and they murmured against Moses and Aaron. They did not realize or trust in the promises of the Lord to care for them, and sustain them in any situation. Periodically, their minds flashed back into the land of Egypt. It is a fact that the nation Israel was redeemed by the power of the Lord, with a stretched-out arm, and with great judgment (6:6-7).

Step by step, God led his chosen people safely towards the noted mountain of God. Indeed, Moses was familiar (3:1) with this noted mountain. The Scripture (Ex. 19:2) tells us they were departed from Rephidim, and were come to the desert of Sinai, and had pitched in the wilderness; and Israel camped before the mount. Moses was called (19:1-7; Acts 7:38-39) to God's presence at Sinai, "Ye have seen what I did unto the Egyptians, and how I bare you on eagle's wings, and brought you unto myself. Now therefore, if ye will obey my voice indeed, and keep my covenant, then ye shall be a peculiar treasure unto me above all people: for the earth is mine. And all the people answered together, and said: All that the Lord hath spoken we will do. And Moses returned the words of the people unto the Lord."

God related to Moses how He had redeemed Israel out from bondage in the land of Egypt. The designation of God's terms or conditions indicate God's purpose and desire to establish (Ex. 19:5-6) a spiritual relationship with Israel is noted. "And ye shall be unto me a kingdom of priests, and an holy nation." Israel was redeemed by the divine power of God. The Exodus of Israel, was indeed, an act of redemption, by the mighty hand of God (Deut. 7:8).

Moses prepared Israel (Ex. 19:7-25) for the law; the law was given (20:1-26) at Sinai. The law was added (Gal. 3:19) because of transgression. Wherefore the law is holy, and the commandment is holy, and just, and good (Rom. 7:12). Indeed, the law leads to Christ (Gal. 3:24-25), nonetheless, the law could not remove sin. (Heb. 9:9-15 Gal. 3:19-20) tells us, wherefore then serveth the law? It was added because of transgression, till the seed should come to whom the promise was made; and it was ordained by angels in the hand of a mediator. Now a mediator is not a mediator of one, but God is one. God is the lawgiver, Moses was the (John 7:19) lawgiver. Rom. 3:20 tells us the law magnifies sin.

The law was called (Deut. 4:13, 23) a covenant; the law was dedicated (Heb. 9:18-22) by the blood. The essence of life (Lev. 17:11, 14) is in the blood.

The Old Testament is explicitly a divine religion of law commanded by God, for all mankind. The Ten Commandments (Ex. 20:) were written with the finger (32:16) of God. The Scripture (James 2:10) tells us that whosoever shall keep the whole law, and yet offend in one point, "he is guilty of all." Indeed, only exclusive worship is pleasing to God.

Moses had prepared Israel, God's redeemed treasure, to hear and see the miracles of God from the top of the mount. And Moses brought forth the people (Ex. 19:17) out of the camp to meet with God; and they stood at the nether part of the mount. The Scripture (v. 18) tells us the whole mount quaked greatly. And the Lord (v. 20) came down upon Mount Sinai, on the top of the mount.

The people heard (Ex. 20:1-17) the voice (Deut. 5:22-33) of God, as He spoke from the top of the mount. The people were very fearful; begged that God's voice be heard no more, lest they die. "And so terrible was the sight, that Moses said, I exceedingly fear and quake."

Moses received the law at Mount Sinai. Moses related the law to the people. The Israelites (Ex. 19:1-25) promised to obey the law and the covenant. The covenant (19:5) was a spiritual agreement between God and man, instituted at Mt. Sinai. The covenant (24:6-8) was ratified. The blood is noted. "And almost all things are by the law purged with blood; and without shedding of blood is no remission" (Heb. 9:22). The passover (Ex. 12:3-28) was instituted. The passover was observed (Num. 9:1-14) at Mount Sinai in the wilderness. The sacred reflection of each passover brings to mind the fact, the institution (Ex. 12:1-14) of the passover, the last passover meal down in the land of Egypt. The blood was a token upon the houses where the Israelites were dwelling. Indeed, the applying of the blood (vs. 6-7) was very, very necessary. There is power in the cleansing blood. The essence of life (Lev. 17:11) is in the blood (atonement). When I see the blood, I will pass over you. The Lord's presence was always with His chosen people. The destroyer, the angel of death, did not smite the firstborn of the Jewish people. The sign on the houses was surrounded by the meaning of the passover. The blood (Lev. 17:10-14) is the means of atonement.

The people understood the meaning of animal sacrifice as a mean of atonement (Lev. 16:11, 14-22) for guilt, the forgiveness of sin, the reconciliation of the guilty by divine sacrifice. Indeed, the sacrifices were substitutional as shadows, symbols, and types. These were established preparative methods. Through the grace of our God, all the demands were met and fulfilled (John 19:30) at Calvary.

The Bible unfolds numerous narratives revealing the love and the merciful hand of God. It is noted that man's relationship with God began publicly (Gen. 4:4), early in the Old Testament. The Israelites, God's chosen people, had observed many, many miracles of God: The exodus from bondage in Egypt, the journey from the Red Sea to Sinai. They saw the glory of the Lord, the cloud, and the fire of God that led them day and night through the wilderness. The Israelites were aware of the presence of the Lord, still, they were disobedient to God's law, and the law of Moses, who was God's earthy representative in the spiritual leadership of Israel and the exodus of God's chosen people. It is a fact that we are sometimes visible examples (Ex. 14-10) of the Israelites. We seek God's help when we realize the fact that we are helpless creatures without His mercy. "The Creator (Rom. 1:20), (Acts 5:29) is merciful, worthy to be praised."

Through the leadership of Moses, the religion of God's new redeemed nation was disclosed. God's covenant (Ex. 19:5; 24:6-8) with Israel is noted.

The Ten Commandments made possible many functions through divine authority, providing the available means that were essential reflections in the minds of God's new (Deut. 6:1-18) redeemed people. It was very important for the new nation Israel to fellowship with their Redeemer, noting the building of the tabernacle, enabling God's chosen people to worship Him as desired. Let us keep in mind, the nation Israel started with one man. The call (Gen. 12:1-3) of Patriarch Abraham, noting (v. 3). (Acts 7:6-38).

It is noted that both Moses and Aaron were wholly aware of the fact (Num. 20:8-12) that they would not bring this congregation that left out of Egypt into the Promised Land. Miriam's death (20:1) is noted. Aaron's death (20:24) is noted. All of the people that were twenty years of age or older at the time of Israel's deliverance (Exodus) from Egypt, their fate was to be consumed in the wilderness, except Joshua and Caleb (32:10-14, 26:63-65).

God promised to bless the Israelites if they would be obedient to God's commandments, nonetheless, the host did not wholly commit themselves to God in faith, they were a stiff-necked people, disobedient, and rebellious murmuring people against the Lord God and Moses.

The golden calf (Ex. 32:) is noted. Israel committed a great sin. Step by step, Moses related the words of the Lord to the people; they were aware of blessings if they obeyed the commandments of God. They were also aware of the consequences (Deut. 28:2, 15) if they did not obey God. "And the people spake against God, and against Moses: Wherefore have ye brought us up out of Egypt to die in the wilderness? for there is no bread, neither is there any water; and our soul loatheth this light bread." Indeed, God was angry with His chosen people. God is angry with us today, if we are not obedient to His word. Israel received the law by the disposition of angels, and have not kept it (Acts 7:51-53). We are sometimes examples of the Israelites. In the Old Testament, God demanded exclusive worship; God demands the same of us today. "For if God spared not His angels that sinned, but cast them down to hell, and delivered them into chains of darkness, to be reserved unto judgment." But he that doeth wrong shall receive for the wrong which he hath done and there is no respect of persons. (Col. 3:25).

Through the deliverance (Exodus) of Israel, untold influence gave rise to Israel's religion. Profound sacred history noting the last passover (Ex. 12) meal pointing to the New Testament in type: "Christ comes to mind, as the Lamb of God without blemish." The Last Supper comes to mind (Mat. 26:17; John 1:29; 1 Pet. 1:19). Indeed, the offering of sacrifice was approved by God. It is noted that man's relationship with God began publicly (Gen. 4:4), early in the Old Testament (Heb. 11:4). The priesthood and spiritual sacrifices are noted (Ex. 28:1). He that sacrificeth unto any god, save unto the Lord only, he shall be utterly destroyed. The blood of the sacrificial animal (applied), illustrated a future spiritual image in the eyes and in the minds of the true believers (I Cor. 5:7; St. John 19:30; Heb. 9:22).

From the Book of Genesis to the Book of Revelation, it is noted, "Christ is the Principle Theme of the Bible."

Indeed, we are aware, that the Old Testament sacrifices were "shadows," types exercised as a preparatory mean that the guilty might observe the foreshadow of God's redemptive plan, and grasp the reality, realizing that there was forgiveness (atonement) for sins. "...For it is the blood that maketh an atonement for the soul...."

Moses was indeed faithful (Num. 12:7) in the house of the Lord. Moses believed (Heb. 11:23-28) strongly in the God of Patriarch Abraham, Isaac and Jacob, relying on His Word.

Again, both Moses and Aaron were aware (Num. 20:1-12) of the fact they would not lead this congregation that came up out of Egypt into the Promised Land. It is a fact that man must obey God. He speaks in many ways today, revealing His existence, and His mighty power. God is the same yesterday, and today, and forever.

Through the mighty hand of God, The Exodus of Israel from slavery was simply a divine act of redemption.

Before closing the Pentateuch, it is important to reiterate the history and the background of Israel. Abram was divinely called (Gen. 12:1-3) and tested for specific purposes. Indeed, God was aware of Abram's whole being, noting the fact that Abram would be trustworthy, obedient, and willing to do His will. Abram's name was later changed (17:5) to Abraham. The covenant with Abraham (Gen. 15:18) is noted. It was through Abraham and his descendants that the Hebrew nation originated, noting that Jacob, one of the sons of Isaac, was the father of the twelve patriarchs (Acts 7:1-39). God raised up his prophets through Israel. Jacob's name (Gen. 35:10) was changed to Israel, who was the father of the twelve tribes of Israel. Is. 43:21 tells us, "This people have I formed for myself; they shall show forth my praise."

Again, the promises were made to Abraham and his seed. Abraham was obedient to God's call. The promise (Gen. 17:4-5) of many descendants, noting God's desire to establish an everlasting covenant between Abraham (15:18), and his seed after him. God foreknew Abraham's capabilities that would lead to divine spiritual leadership, an example from generation to generation. God's spiritual (22:18) promise to Abraham is noted, (Gal. 3:6, 8, 16). The seed of the woman (Gen. 3:15) is noted. The promised seed (12:1-3) is noted, (Gal. 3:16). Salvation was announced to Abraham who was a man of steadfast faith. The Abrahamic (Gal. 3:17-18) covenant is a covenant of faith. Through God's spiritual promise of grace, at God's appointed time, Christ would be born into the world (Mat. 1:1, 20-21) as patriarch Abraham's descendant of the tribe (Gen. 49:10; Heb. 7:14) of Judah.

Gal. 3:7 tells us, "Know ye therefore that they which are of faith, the same are the children of Abraham." Vs. 8-9 tells us, "...In thee shall all nations be blessed...." So then they which be of faith are blessed with faithful Abraham. Heb. 11:17 tells us that by faith Abraham, when he was tried, offered up Isaac, and he that had received the promises offered up his only begotten son. Abraham was truly a spiritual influence; an example for all generations to reach out, and stand on the foundation of faith. It is noted that Abraham was forewarned (Gen. 15:13-14) of Israel's bondage in Egypt. God foresaw the need for an earthly liberator. Centuries passed; at God's appointed time, a baby was born (Ex. 2:1-24). In due time, a liberator named Moses was divinely called (3:1-7), noting the burning bush. Moses was God's chosen one to lead the children of Israel out of bondage in Egypt. Moses was a great leader, and a great servant of God. "And there arose not a prophet since in Israel like unto Moses, whom the Lord knew face to face."

Moses was aware that he would not go over Jordan (Deut. 4:21-24) into the good land, the land of promise (Num. 20:8-12). Moses warned the people (Deut. 8:11-18) against forgetting the Lord. "We are sometimes examples of the Israelites." The Scripture (Deut. 3:26-28) tells us Moses viewed the Promised Land. "So Moses the servant of the Lord died there in the land of Moab, according to the word of the Lord."

At the time of Moses' death, Joshua had been a minister under Moses. Joshua was divinely appointed and consecrated as the successor to Moses. All of the host that came up out of Egypt at the time of the Exodus (Num. 32:10-13) were consumed in the wilderness. Of this host, only Kaleb (v. 12) and Joshua entered the Promised Land. The Scripture (Deut. 31:23) tells us, "And he gave Joshua the son of Num a charge, and said: Be strong and of good courage: for thou shall bring the children of Israel into the land which I sware unto them: and I will be with thee."

Obedience to the Faith

"And ye shall be unto me a kingdom of priests and an holy nation. These are the words which thou shalt speak unto the children of Israel (Ex. 19:6)." God demands total obedience.

The Scriptures (Gen. 14:18) tell us that Melchezedek was the priest of the Most High God. Ex. 3:1 tells us Jethro was the priest of Midian during the time of Israel's bondage down in Egypt. During the patriarchal age it is noted that before the law was given, the heads of families performed or offered sacrifice, who was the family priest. Is. 61:6 tells us, "But ye shall be named the Priests of the Lord: men shall call you the Ministers of our God: ye shall eat the riches of the Gentiles and in their glory shall ye boast yourselves." Holiness is of God. There were many duties and requirements of the priests.

The purification of the priests is noted. The offering of the sacrifices was required by the priests (Lev. 1:1-11). Indeed, there were restrictions for the priesthood (10:8-9). Step by step, God was revealing His holy purpose, esteeming the essentialities of His redemptive plan for His people.

In due time, at God's appointed time, we note in the New Testament Christ's Priesthood (Heb. 9:11-12). The new covenant (Heb. 8:6-13) obtained a more excellent ministry in days to come (Jer. 31:32-34). For if that first covenant had been faultless, then should no place have been sought for the second. (Heb. 10:11-18) tells us, noting (vs. 11, 12), that every priest standeth daily ministering and offering often times the same sacrifices, which can never take away sins. But this man, after He had offered one sacrifice for sins forever, sat down at the right hand of God, "For by one offering He hath perfected for ever them that are sanctified." Indeed, the new covenant is unerring. "There is one redemption." The foundation of the new covenant is bound by the blood of Jesus Christ. Eternal salvation (redemption) was obtained for us because Christ sacrificed Himself for us.

Before coming to the end of the priests and the Old Testament sacrifices, it is noted that there were priests functioning before the law (Ex. 3:1-2) was given at Mount Sanai. The Old Testament sacrifices (Gen. 4:4; Heb. 11:4) were truly approved by God. The priests were publicly (Ex. 28:1) set apart by the Lord. "Wherefore the law is holy, and the commandment holy, and just, and good." It is a fact that the law (Rom. 3:20; Gal. 3:24-26, 4:4) fulfilled the divine purposes of God. The priesthood of Israel was God's own people. "But you are a chosen generation, a royal priesthood, a holy nation, a peculiar people; that ye should show forth the praise of Him who hath called you out of darkness into His marvelous light.

The word sacrifice embraces the ancient records of Israel's history, noting the blood of the sacrificial animals as types, shadows of the real things to come, Christ Himself.

The Prophets and Prophetess

"And it shall come to pass afterward, that I will pour out my spirit upon all flesh; and your sons and daughters shall prophesy, your old men shall dream dreams, your young men shall see visions."

The prophets were God's inspired messengers (II Chr. 36:15-16), the holy men (II Pet. 1:20-21) of God. The last words of David are noted, who was a man after God's own heart. The Spirit of the Lord spake by me, and His word was in my tongue. The prophets unfold God's messages to the people of its present and future preparation; their missions were wholly given to them by God, "they were moved by the Holy Ghost."

The prophets of God were divinely designated to speak forth to the people for God. The true prophets could clearly see, or discern through visions or dreams through the revelation of God. Prophetic insight was given to the prophets to religiously teach, giving divine guidance to the people as God had given the revelation to them. The people were informed, or reminded of future promises to come.

The prophets warned the nation of dangers or evils that could harm the people, or the course of their journey should be changed to another direction. The people were aware of the things (Deut. 29:29) that belonged to them, noting the fulfilling of future things to come.

God informed His prophets by means of dreams, visions or darkness, making them aware of His will to be activated by/or through their missions. Through the utterance or utterances of the prophets, they were speaking for God, relating to the people the things (Deut. 29:29) God wanted them to know. The prophets were divinely inspired to deliver to the nation the inspired messages of God; they were moved by the Holy Ghost.

The prophets were motivated by divine influence. It is perceived that the people looked forward, grasping into the unknown by faith, hope, and assurance in the promises of God. It is a fact that God's plan of redemption for the future of mankind can be spiritually discerned.

Looking back into the Old Testament, noting the priestly rituals, perceiving the blood of the animals that were slain and sacrificed for atonement, the forgiveness of sins. Those sacrifices were important, they meant much in the eyes and in minds of the guilty. It was understood, through those sacrifices, there was atonement for sins. The blood upon the altar produced the desired effect (Lev. 4:23-26). It is a fact that those sacrifices could not atone for man's sins. The sacrifices were types (shadows), foreshadowing good heavenly things to come (propitiatory), at God's appointed time. Step by step, God leads us into His divine way, into the light of His redemptive plan for salvation (Eph. 1:3-7). "Neither by the blood of goats and calves" but by His own blood He entered in once into the holy place, having obtained eternal redemption for us "noting (Heb. 9:12, 22, Rom. 3:25)."

The Scripture (Ex. 28:1) tells us Aaron was chosen by God for the priesthood, also his four sons were priests. It is noted that Aaron was designated as the first priest under Moses. The garments for the priests (vs. 2-14) are noted. Some of the duties of priests are noted-a person whose function is to make sacrificial offerings and perform other religious rites. The priests were working on missions authorized and approved by the Lord (30:30), and for the Lord. Moses, the brother of Aaron, committed the written law to the priests. Indeed, God purposed and approved the offering of sacrifices. Each animal sacrifice, noting the blood, were types, still, true believers might look back and visualize the sacrificing of Christ Himself for us. "Redemption was God's plan."

God had purposes for His prophets. A prophet is a person who speaks for God by divine guidance. The prophets were holy men, working and speaking for God. Some prophets were preachers, teachers, who taught religion among the people; and some prophets predicted future events to come centuries before they occurred. It is obvious to note the true prophets related only the things that God had related to them, to relate to the people. In fact, the prophets were prophetically moved by the Holy Ghost.

God warned His prophets to be aware of false prophets, and their messages of prophecies, that they might warn the nation of their false teachings. The prophets served as great leaders for the nation. The prophets were spiritually potently strong, and dedicated to God.

Among the ancient schools of the prophets, the students were noted as sons of the prophets. Some ancient biblical history was made known from generation to generation by and through God's inspired holy men, the prophets. The prophets served in powerful positions, as mediators between God and the nation. They were indeed speaking for God, relating the messages of God to the nation. It is a fact that God speaks to us today in so many ways. We tend to recognize the works of God, and the power of God, when we are in situations that leave us totally helpless, with no one else to turn to, except God. It is indeed wise, and right, to acknowledge Him: (Prov. 3:5-7). Prov. 9:11 tells us, "For by me thy days shall be multiplied, and the years of thy life shall be increased. The fear of the Lord is the beginning of wisdom," and (21:2) tells us that every way of a man is right in his own eyes, but the Lord pondereth the hearts.

Some of the doctrine related by the prophets was false, which was never effective. Nonetheless, God is aware of all things at the same time. Jer. 5:31 tells us the prophets prophecy falsely, and the priests bear rule by their means; and my people love to have it so: and what will ye do in the end thereof? Some of the priests were prophets also (Ezek. 1:3). The ministry of some of the Prophets expounded repentance, judgment, and obedience.

Moses was a great prophet, who was committed to do the divine will of God. Moses focused not upon himself, but gave his utmost to do God's will. It was Moses who brought the Children of Israel out of Egypt, by the way of the Red Sea to Mount Sinai where the people heard God's voice. It was on this mountain that God revealed His existence and His presence to His new nation. Moses received (Ex. 20:1-26) the law at Sinai. Ex. 33:11 tells us, "And the Lord spake unto Moses face to face as a man speaketh unto his friend. "Moses was a type of Christ. It was through the prophet Moses that Israel's religion was made a reality, and was revealed to the people. The promised Prophet is noted, "The Lord thy God will raise up unto thee a Prophet from the midst of thee, of thy brethren, like unto me; unto him ye shall hearken." Moses was a faithful servant over God's house. Deut. 34:10 tells us "And there arose not a prophet since in Israel like unto Moses whom the Lord knew face to face."

It is noted that there were prophetess' who did exercise the prophetic gift in ancient Israel, the early Christians, and the early church is noted. Miriam was the sister of Moses (Ex. 15:20), who was an active prophetess. Indeed, there were other women who were active in the early churches.

Lastly, the eternal promises and the prophecies of the Old Testament are noted. The first promise (Gen. 3:15) of a Redeemer is noted, seed of woman (Gal. 4:4). The promised seed (Gen. 12:1-3) is noted (Gal. 3:16). The same promise (3:15) was repeated to Abraham (22:18), the man of faith. It was given to David also, noting (II Sam. 7:12; 13; 28). Abraham's faith (Rom. 4:13, 16) is noted (Gen. 17:15-19). "Please note the divine mystery." Through Shem's descendants (Gen. 11:26), the promised Messiah was expected to come. Shem was the oldest son of Noah. The promise was announced (12:1-3; 17:15-19; 22:18) to Abraham, then to Isaac. It is noted that Abraham's faith (Gen. 22:) was tested. Nonetheless, it was a divine fact. Isaac was the designated one through whom the Messiah was to come. "The sacrifice of the Messiah for the redemption of all mankind." Esau and Jacob were the sons of Isaac, who was the son of Abraham. Jacob was the father of the twelve tribes of Israel. Jacob's prophecy concerning his son is noted (49:10). The scepter shall not depart from Judah, nor a lawgiver from between his feet, until Shiloh come, noting (Num. 24:17). The Messiah was a star out of Jacob, of Judah's tribe, of David's seed (Mat. 1:1). "I have made a covenant with my chosen, I have sworn unto David my servant; Thy seed will I establish for ever, and build up thy throne to all generations." Please note: (Ps. 89:3-4).

It was through the prophets that the people were in the foreknowledge of the promised Messiah; Moses' law is noted. Luke 24:44 tells us, "And he said unto them, These are the words which I spake unto you, while I was yet with you, that all things must be fulfilled, which were written in the law of Moses, and in the prophets, and in the psalms, concerning Me. I will raise them up a Prophet from among their brethren: like unto thee, and will put my words in his mouth; and he shall speak unto them all that I shall command him."

It is noted that the blessings of patriarch Abraham was passed down the line to his descendants, noting (Gen. 12:2, 21:12, 25:23-24). Through Abraham, blessings for the whole world (12:3) were made possible. The promises were made to patriarch Abraham and his seed. "And in thee shall all families of the earth be blessed." Please note: (Gal. 3:16). God was wholly aware that Abraham had the needed qualities, noting his faith, to become the father of the nation, noting (Gen. 22:). "At God's appointed time, the promised Savior will come to redeem the lost souls." Redemption was God's plan.

The prophets' prophetical messages were not only for the people of their time, but for generations to come. The prophets expounded the work of the coming Messiah, "the anointed," who is to reign on David's throne. It is noted that Isaac was indeed the one through whom the Messiah was to come, noting the Jewish tribe of Judah (Gen. 49:10). Is. 7:14 tells us, "Therefore the Lord Himself shall give you a sign; Behold, a virgin shall conceive, and bear a son, and shall call His name

Immanuel." Of which salvation the prophets have inquired and searched diligently, who prophesied of the grace that should come unto you. "...My grace is sufficient for thee...."

There were many Masianic prophecies, events, and objects that were noted as parallels to Christ, noting the ark (Gen. 7:13). Gen. 3:21 tells us that the Lord made garments of skin for Adam and his wife, and clothed them.

The promise of the Messiah was indeed a part of the messages of the prophets, noting (Deut. 18:15-19). There were women (Acts 21:9, I Cor. 11:5) that prophesied, they were active in the churches of God.

The Messiah was present from the beginning. The Messiah (Word) was an agent in the creation of the heaven and the earth, and all that exists, noting (John 1:1). "Who is the image of the invisible God-the firstborn of every creature," (Col. 1:15). "The Word was always with God." God's redemptive plan of salvation is possible only through the Son of God. "He that believeth on the Son hath everlasting life: and he that believeth not the Son shall not see life; but the wrath of God abideth on him." Through the messages of the prophets, the people were aware of the good things to come through the Messiah. "His redemptive work was made known then, and that same redemption of Christ is eternal."

In due time, at God's appointed time, the Messiah takes on Himself the form of a man, to be revealed as the Son of man, the center of divine power and glory. The Messiah, as the Son of Man, is a preexistent heavenly being. Let us note the words of Jesus, "Verly, verly, I say unto you-Before Abraham was, I am," noting (John 1:1).

But thou, Bethlehem Ephratah, though thou be little among the thousands of Judah, yet out of thee shall He come forth unto me that is to be ruler in Israel; whose goings forth have been from old, from everlasting (Micah 5:2)."

At God's appointed time, Christ the true Messiah was divinely sent into the world, bringing in everlasting righteousness to save sinners, to destroy Satan's work, to give life, fulfill the Old Testament, and to do God's will.

chapter 7

Christ Fulfilled the Prophecies

"Therefore the Lord Himself shall give you a sign: Behold a virgin shall conceive, and bear a son, and shall call His name Immanuel (Is. 7:14). To a virgin espoused to a man whose name was Joseph, of the house of David; and the virgin's name was Mary. (Luke 1:27-28).

"And she shall bring forth a son, and thou shall call his name JESUS: for he shall save his people from their sins." Jesus was conceived by the Holy Ghost. He was born of a virgin birth in Bethlehem of Judea in the days of Herod the king. Behold, there came wise men from the east to Jerusalem, noting (Mat. 1:21, 2:1-3, 13). King Herod was very troubled when he was informed about the young child. He sought means to destroy the young child; the place of Jesus' birth was indeed in question. Let us note that throughout the Old Testament, God spake to the prophets about the coming of the Messiah, also the place of His birth (Mic. 5:2) was made known.

It is a fact that God is aware of all secrets. He knows the thoughts of all mankind. He is a discerner of the hearts of men. God warned the wise men in a dream they were instructed to travel in another direction, back to their country. It is a fact that Harod sought to destroy the young child. Nonetheless, the prophecy of the coming of the Messiah was divinely fulfilled, at God's appointed time. "For unto us a child is born, unto us a Son is given: and the government shall be upon his shoulder: and his name shall be called Wonderful, Counselor: The Mighty God: The everlasting Father: The Prince of Peace" (Is. 9:6). Jesus was named by the angel before He was conceived in the womb, noting (Luke 2:21-22).

The child grew strong, filled with divine wisdom, and the grace of God was upon Him. At age twelve, Jesus was found in the temple by his parents. He was in the midst of doctors, lawyers, and many great leaders, hearing them, and asking them questions. Those that heard Him could not believe what they were hearing; they were astonished at the understanding of Jesus, noting the questions that Jesus answered.

Jesus was baptized by John the Baptist. He was anointed for divine service. St. Luke 3:21-22 tells us, "Now when all the people were baptized, it came to pass, that Jesus also being baptized, and praying, the heaven was opened: And the Holy Ghost descended in a bodily shape like a dove upon Him, and a voice came from heaven, which said, Thou art my beloved Son; in thee I am well pleased." Jesus was led out into the wilderness by the Holy Spirit to be tempted of the devil, nonetheless, each time the temptation came, Jesus spoke divine words. "Get thee behind me Satan: for it is written, Thou shalt worship the Lord thy God, and Him only shalt thou serve."

In the beginning was the Word, and the Word was with God, and the Word was God. "And all things were made by Him; and without Him was not any thing made that was made." Jesus was God in the flesh (Eph. 3:4-5; 9). "Jesus was made of a woman, made under the law (Ga. 4:4)." Jesus was in the world, (John 1:10) and the world was made by Him, and the world knew Him not. Jesus was born not of blood, nor of the will of the flesh, nor of the will of man, but of God. "...And the word was made flesh, and dwelt among us...." Please note: (vs. 11-17). John 1:1 tells us, "In the beginning was the Word, and the Word was with God, and the Word was God."

Jesus was about thirty years old when He began His public ministry. He tought multitudes of people. "He walked upon the deep waters of Galilee: The winds and the waves obeyed His command: He healed the sick and He raised the dead. He gave sight to the blind, and hearing to the deaf. He cast out demons and made the lame to walk. He turned water into wine, and fed five thousand with five loaves of bread and two fishes."

It is a fact that God loves us all the same, with an everlasting love. "But God commendeth His love toward us, in that, while we were yet sinners, Christ died for us." Being justified freely by His grace through the redemption that is in Christ Jesus, whom God hath set forth to be a propitiation through faith in His blood to declare his righteousness for the remission of sins that are passed through the forbearance of God. Salvation was planned (Eph. 1:4-12) in eternity. Salvation was announced (Gen. 3:15) from the beginning. "For God so loved the world, that He gave His only begotten Son, that whosoever believeth in Him should not perish, but have everlasting life." The prophets made known to the nation, the prophetic promises of the Messiah (Gen. 3:15; 12:3; Gal. 3:16) ages before the birth of Jesus.

Early in Jesus' ministry, He called men out of the world to become fishers of men. The past lives of the men were not an important factor if they were willing to follow Jesus and obey His teachings. Indeed, following in the footsteps of the Son of God, it is conceivable to deem the fact that if the men were willing to follow Jesus; these men were sure to become spiritually influenced by divine power. "Faith comes by hearing, (Rom. 10:17) and hearing the Word of God." Looking unto Jesus the author and finisher of our faith.

Jesus preached the gospel of the kingdom of God, and saying, "The time is fulfilled, and the kingdom of God is at hand: repent ye, and believe the gospel." Jesus tought His disciples the need for steadfast faith. Jesus performed many miracles. There were Jews converted, and baptized. Many people witnessed the healing power of Jesus, and the saving power of Jesus. They were so impressed that they related to others the miracles they had seen Jesus perform, noting the Chief priests, and the Pharisees who refused to except the Son of Man was Lord the Christ. Indeed, they were spiritually blind to things, they were the separated ones.

The plot to kill Jesus is noted. The High Priest (Mat. 26:27:28:) felt that Jesus should die. He was hated by many without cause. Jesus was betrayed by one of the twelve for thirty pieces of silver (Mat. 26:14-16).

The Last Supper is observed, "And as they were eating, Jesus took bread, and blessed it, and broke it, and gave it to the disciples, and said: "Take, eat; this is my body." And He took the cup, and gave thanks, and gave it to them, saying, "Drink ye all of it; For this is my blood of the New Testament, which is shed for many for the remission of sins." (Mat. 26:17-28).

Jesus was wholly aware that He would be betrayed; He also knew who His betrayer would be. Jesus was also aware that Peter (vs. 31-35) would deny Him before the cock crow.

"And Jesus going up to Jerusalem took the twelve disciples apart in the way, and said unto them: Behold, we go up to Jerusalem; and the Son of Man shall be betrayed unto the chief priests, and unto the scribes, and they shall condemn Him to death: And shall deliver Him to the Gentiles to mock and to scourge, and to crucify Him, (Mat. 20:17-19; see Mark 10:32, 34 NIV) and the third day He shall rise again." Jesus was foretelling His passion.

The Scripture tells us that Jesus was hated without cause. Satan entered into Judas, who was the betrayer, who betrayed Jesus (Mat. 26:47-50) with a kiss. There in the garden of Gethsemane, the multitude came with swords and staves, and Judas said, Hail, master, and kissed Him, that the multitude seeking Jesus would hold Him fast.

Jesus was taken before (Mat. 26:-27:) the high priest, and the chief-priest took Jesus to Pilate. Please note (Is. 53:7). Jesus was sentenced to die. "The governor asked the question, Why, What evil hath He done?" Jesus was taken away, scourged, and delivered to be crucified. The Scripture tells us, "...Jesus had related to His disciples the fact He would be leaving, and the coming Comforter would ever be with them. Jesus was aware that the disciples' hearts were filled with sorrow (John 16:4-15): Step by step, Jesus spoke comforting words to them, noting the foretelling of His passion (please note John 14:15-27).

The Scriptures tells us, "...Jesus stood before the governor, and the governor asked Jesus saying: Art thou the King of the Jews? And Jesus said unto him-Thou sayest...." Pilate saith unto them (the multitude); What shall I do then with Jesus which is called the Christ? They all said unto him, Let him be crucified. (Mat. 27:11, 22). Please note: (John 6:38-43).

Then delivered he Him therefore unto them to be crucified. And they took Jesus, and led Him away. The Scripture tells us, "As many were astonied at thee: His visage was so marred more than any man, and His form more than the sons of men." (Is. 52:14, NIV). "He was oppressed, and He was afflicted: yet He opened not His mouth: He is brought as a lamb to the slaughter, and as a sheep before her shearers is dumb, so He openeth not His mouth" (53:7-12, NIV). "Indeed, Jesus was God in the flesh."

God's love (John 3:16) for the world was/is unlimited, that everlasting love for us was/is so solemnly offered, and profoundly demonstrated throughout the whole world. There is never a shortage of God's love, and He is wholly aware of those that truly love Him. Through the hours of intense suffering. "Father-forgive them; for they know not what they do (Luke 23:24-38)." Jesus was willing to sacrifice Himself for the sins of the world (Heb. 9:22-28), noting (vs. 25-26).

The main principle mission of Jesus' coming into the world was to be born as the Savior of the world (Luke 2:11), as only the atoning blood of Christ (Rom. 3:24-25); (Col. 1:14) could atone for the sins of the world, only through divine sacrifice.

The Scripture tells us Jesus was led away to be crucified (John 19:16-30). "...Jesus was bearing His cross, went forth into a place called the place of the skull, which is called in the Hebrew Golgotha..."

"...Then the soldiers, when they had crucified Jesus, took His garments, and made four parts, to every soldier a part; and also His coat...." (Ps. 22:18) tells us, "They part my garments among them, and cast lots upon my vesture."

"After this, Jesus knowing that all things were now accomplished, that the Scripture might be fulfilled, saith, I thirst. Vinegar was offered to Jesus. When Jesus therefore had received the vinegar, He said, It is finished: and He bowed His head, and gave up the ghost" (John 19:16-30).

The soldiers pierced Jesus in His side with a spear. The Scripture tells us, "...and forthwith came there out blood and water...." The burial of Jesus (vs. 38-42) is noted. The first day of the week cometh Mary Magdalene early, when it was yet dark, unto the sepulcher, and seeth the stone taken away from the sepulcher (20:). Mary Magdalene ran to find the disciples, whom Jesus loved, and told them, "They have taken away the Lord out of the sepulcher, and we know not where they have laid Him."

Periodically, Jesus had foretold (Mat. 20:17-19) His disciples that He would be crucified, and on the third day He shall rise again (Mat. 16:21). Jesus warned His disciples of His persecution (passion). Jesus also related to His disciples that He would be leaving, and the coming Comforter would show them the right way, noting the fact that it would be an advantage for Him to leave them. "Nevertheless, I tell you the truth; It is expedient for you that I go away, :for if I go not away, the Comforter will not come unto you; but if I depart, I will send Him unto you." The disciples were saddened, they only understood some of the words that Jesus had related to them concerning His leaving them.

Indeed, their hearts were filled with joy when they learned that Jesus had been seen, He had truly risen from the dead, and had appeared unto Mary Magdalene (John 20:-21:). Some of the disciples had seen Jesus. Mat. 28:16-20 tells us that then the eleven disciples went away into Galilee, into a mountain where Jesus had appointed them. The Scripture tells us that Jesus came and spake unto them, saying, "All power is given unto Me in heaven and earth."

Jesus told His disciples to go in all nations, teaching, and baptizing in the name of the Father, and of the Son, and of the Holy Ghost. Jesus related to His disciples, "...I am with you always, even unto the end of the world. Amen...."

Repentance was preached (Mark 1:1-4) by John the Baptist in the Old Testament, before the birth of Christ. Repentance was preached during the life and ministry of Christ, and it was also preached on the day of Pentecost. Indeed, that same repentance is preached in our midst today. John preached saying, "There cometh one mightier than I after me, the latchet of whose shoes I am not worthy to stoop down and unloose (vs. 7-8)."

After the resurrection of Christ, the fears of the disciples vanished and they had acquired none wavering courage, hope, and faith within themselves, ready to go in all the world, expounding the resurrection of Christ. Jesus commanded the twelve on their mission: And as ye go, preach, saying: "The kingdom of heaven is at hand." (Mat. 10:5-8). "Jesus came not to call the righteous, but sinners to repentance."

Jesus assembled with the disciples, and commanded them that they should not depart from Jerusalem, but wait for the promise of the Father, which saith He, ye have heard of me (Acts 1:4-8). "But ye shall receive power, after that the Holy Ghost is come upon you: and ye shall be witnessed unto me both in Jerusalem, and in all Judea, and Samaria, and unto the uttermost part of the earth." (Acts 1:8-14).

The Ascension of Christ is noted and the second coming of Christ is noted. "And when He had spoken these things, while they beheld, He was taken up; and a cloud received Him out of their sight." Please note: (vs. 9-11). Christ instructed His disciples for forty days. After the ascension of Christ up on high, the Scripture (Heb. 10:12) tells us, "But this man, after He had offered one sacrifice for sins forever, sat down on the right hand of God." The promise of the Comforter is noted.

The Scripture tells us that after Jesus Christ was taken up and a cloud received Him out of the sight of the men, there were two men that stood by them in white apparel which also said, "Ye men of Galilee, why stand ye gazing up into heaven? This same Jesus, which is taken up from you into heaven, shall so come in like manner as ye have seen Him go into heaven."

The Scripture (Mat. 25:31-46) tells us, "When the Son of Man shall come in His glory, and all the holy angels with Him, then shall He sit upon the throne of glory: And before Him shall be gathered all nations: and He shall separate them one from another, as a shepherd divideth His sheep from the goats." It is noted that from Genesis to Revelation, Christ is the center of the Bible. The Scripture (John 21:25) tells us, "And there are also many other things which Jesus did, the which, if they should be written every one, I suppose that even the world itself could not contain the books that should be written."

On the Day of Pentecost, those who observed the actions of those who were empowered, or filled with the Holy Ghost were speaking in other tongues, as the Spirit gave them utterance. Indeed, some were confused with doubts, and some were amazed. There were others mocking (v. 13) who said, "These men are full of new wine." Peter related to them in his address at the Pentecost, for these are not drunken, as ye suppose, seeing it is but the third hour of the day. It is a fact that the touch or the moving of the Holy Spirit moves one with divine authority. It is from this influence that the Spirit of God is alive (noted), and unites with the human spirit (Acts 2:1-24) within. This is a controlling influence, a force that becomes the seat of one's (Is. 29:10) conscious. From this spiritual unionization, man is able to discern the realities of the true living God. Man's ideas, and daily testimonies become divinely influenced. Man acquires the zeal, and the will to attain spiritual ideas, praying for self and others in the whole world, with steadfast faith in the promises of God, recognizing and willing to obey the laws of God, who is Sovereign. Man was not born with this faith. The Scripture (Rom. 10:17) tells us faith comes by hearing the word. Jesus is the author (Heb. 12:1-2), and finisher of our faith.

It is conceivable to believe, that on the Day of Pentecost, those who were prayerful, awaiting to receive the divine power of the Holy Ghost, when the promise of the Father came upon them, those who were in one accord, were filled with power; they were also filled with uncontrollable passion and joy. They had the needed courage to go out in the world, expounding the way (Acts 2:14-42) of salvation, noting (v. 36-39). Nonetheless, it is conceivable for one to believe those who were not spiritually discerned (I. Cor. 2:14), would be confused, and some would have doubts.

At the cross when Jesus said, "It is finished," all things were accomplished. Again, there is one redemption, that redemption was made possible through the death, and the atoning blood of Christ the Son of God. It is only through the power of God, the blood of Jesus Christ, and the grace of God (Eph. 1:7, Rom. 3:24-25) that redemption (Heb. 9:12) was accomplished for us. God's grace is sufficient (II Cor. 12:9) for thee.

Salvation (John 3:16) is the gift of God. Salvation is an individual choice and decision by faith. "...For by grace are you saved (Eph. 2:5, 8) through faith...." The Scripture (Rom. 5:8) tells us, "But God commendeth His love toward us, in that, while we were yet sinners, Christ died for us." Redemption was God's plan (Eph. 1:4-7).

On the Day of Pentecost, the church received power from on high; believers were eager to evangelize out into the world as they wished, expounding the resurrection of

Christ from the grave. The believers were given power and different callings, that they might serve in the name of the Lord. It is the rightful service of the believers to witness in the service of the Lord, Christ Himself, the chief corner stone. Christ is the Head of the body of the church. Christ is, indeed, the church foundation. He is Lord of Lords; He is the King of Kings, He is seated at the right hand of the Father in heaven, ruling, and controlling the whole universe. The Scripture (I Pet. 3:22) tells us, "Who is gone into heaven, and is on the right hand of God: angels and authorities and powers being made subject unto Him."

Again, the church belongs to God. Before the foundation of the world (Rom. 8:28-33), God had a purpose and plan for the lives of mankind in future times to come, according to His will.

Through the early churches, there were prepared dedicated priests and prophets and prophetess, functioning daily among the people, calling many from out in the world, who were willing to follow and work in the harvest of God. Indeed, Jesus called His church out of the world. "And are built upon the foundation (Eph. 2:19-22) of the apostles and the prophets, Jesus Christ Himself being the chief corner stone." And He is the head of the body, the church, who is the beginning, the first born from the dead, that in all things He might have the preeminence.

The function of the churches was very essential. The church of the congregation Israel in the wilderness at Mount Sanai is noted. The animal sacrifices are noted. It was very important that the sacrifices (Gen. 4:4) were to be activated in faith. Under the great leadership of Moses, religion was disclosed in the wilderness at Sanai, within the nation Israel. Indeed, the law (commandments) of the Old Testament was the Word of God. Even though the sacrifices were substitutional, or preparatory, the shedding of blood had a profound meaning in the eyes, and in the mind of the sacrificer. The Scripture (Col. 2:17) tells us, "Which are a shadow of things to come; but the body is of Christ. Think not that I am come to destroy the law, or the prophets: I am not come to destroy, but to fulfill."

All the demands of the law were covered at the cross, noting the death, resurrection, and the atoning blood of Christ. All the demands of the law were entrusted unto Christ, noting (Mat. 28:18). "And Jesus came and spake unto them, saying, All power is given unto Me in heaven and in earth."

Step by step, preparatory (substitutional) means were activated within the functions of the churches. The churches were God's means of accomplishing and bringing about the spiritual knowledge of salvation to all mankind. The apostles and the prophets are noted, (Eph. 2:20-22). The apostles and the prophets are noted in the Scriptures as having a part, or being agents, in the foundation of the church. Many were devoted, wholly dedicated by a solemn act. Many were killed, and an indefinite number were persecuted, nonetheless, they were steadfast in their spiritual opinions. They had the courage to stand up for the church functions for the cause of the Lord. Many of the Prophets were prophetic, predicting, or foreshadowing the future, and relating the messages to the people, the things to come, noting (Is. 7:14). "Therefore the Lord Himself shall give you a sign: Behold, a virgin shall conceive, and bear a Son, and shall call His name Immanuel." God was with His people in the days of old, and God is the same yesterday, and today, and forever. The promises and the prophecies were made known to the people who looked towards Calvary. Today, we can look back in solemness, with gratitude, visioning Calvary. For God so loved the world, that

He gave His only begotten Son, that whosoever believeth in Him should not perish, but have everlasting life. It is a fact that God is love, and He commands that we love one another. Deut. 6:5 tells us, "And thou shalt love the Lord "thy God"with all thine heart, and with all thy soul, and with all thy might." God's love for all mankind is eternal.

In the path of life, we are sometimes faced with problems, unanswered questions or situations, that cause us to ponder both day and night, causing us to realize that God must, and should be, occupying a meaningful place in our lives. Allowing Satan one moment to enter into our lives, that one moment can mar our spiritual fellowship with God, as it is sin (Is. 59:2) that separates us from God. We note that the flesh is prone to weaken, because of spiritual instability.

It is wise to seek divine counsel in everything that we plan to do. Too many aspects in life are viewed and decided from an outward appearance, or pleasing assertions, and are eventually proven to be false or fatal. It is very wise to note that hidden deception can be a noted factor. "Is it wise-or necessary for one to act, and think later?" "Age is not limited."

The evil forces of the world are like the downward force of gravity. It is also very wise to remember that God is with His children at all times, giving them the added strength. Phil. 4:13 tells us, I can do all things through Christ which strengtheneth me. It is important that our minds are stayed on God, who is the Supreme Being, the Creator, the maker and ruler of the whole universe. He is the overseer of man's going out, and man's coming in, and He is ever eager (if requested) to watch over our children at all times. Faith is the key that makes our prayer request complete. "For God hath not given us the spirit (II Tim. 1:7) of fear, but of power, and of love, and of a sound mind.

God requires of mankind to live in obedience to His laws (Ex. 20). The laws were written with the finger (Ex. 32:16) of God. The laws of God are eternal. The Scripture (Mat. 5:18) tells us, "For verily I say unto you, Till heaven and earth pass, one jot or one tittle shall in no wise pass from the law, till all be fulfilled." God commands mankind to love one another, and to forgive one another. For if ye forgive men their trespasses, your heavenly Father will also forgive you. But if ye forgive not men their trespasses, neither will your Father forgive your trespasses. The law is the Word of God, and God's Word is eternal, and God's Word is the light of the world. It appears that the lot of mankind is to reject the laws of God, leaving questions to be answered (Please note I John 1:9-10).

It is wise to note that we are periodically disciplined through the power and Spirit of God because He cares for us, and He is concerned about our well being. God has the power (James 3:5-8) to control mankind, and the tongues of unruly evil. We are chastened by the Word (Heb. 12:5-9) and the Spirit of God. We develop in character and self control through the divine power of discipline, and self discipline, the evidence is noted until the conclusion of life. "Age is not limited."

The Bible truths are made known to human kind throughout the world, instilling spiritual insight, narrating historical background from the Bible truths, that no other books contain. Indeed, the Bible is the greatest Book ever written (Heb. 4:12). The Bible makes known the infallible Word of God. "For the invisible things of Him from the creation of the world are clearly seen, being understood by the things that are made, even His eternal power and God-head; so that they are without excuse." (Please note Acts 15:18; Eph. 3:17.)

The wisdom of God is eternal. The wisdom of God is not of the world. It is the wisdom of the Spirit, which is God uniting with the human spirit of mankind, safeguarding and controlling our going out, and our coming in, still in His protective care. It is the indwelling Spirit, and the power of God that restores our health and strength (Is. 40:31), noting the (Rom. 12:2) renewing of the mind. False wisdom is of the world, which can penetrate into the mind, and is eventually found to be misguiding. The wisdom (I Cor. 3:19) of the world is foolishness to God. It is wise to ponder, convey values, also our ideas, noting the value of knowledge, and the value of understanding. It is a fact that God is the author of knowledge and understanding, and His wisdom (Is. 40:12-28) is unsearchable. "Hast thou not known? hast thou not heard, that the everlasting God, the Lord, the Creator of the ends of the earth, fainteth not, neither is weary? there is no searching of His understanding." Please note: (Eph. 3:10-12). In whom we have boldness and access with confidence by the faith of Him.

In the path of life, the evil forces are very visible, periodically appearing to be on the rise. Mark 4:15 tells us, "And these are they by the way side, where the Word is sown; but when they have heard, Satan cometh immediately and taketh away the Word that was sown in their hearts." It is impossible to be misled by the Word of God, His counsel is mine, and sound wisdom. I am understanding, I have strength. I have faith, I have hope, and I trust in God, and His holy Word.

It is wise to pray for guidance with divine faith. Jesus prayed time after time, He tought His disciples to pray. The prayers of and with faith prevaileth much (Jas. 5:15-16). Ps. 5:8 tells us, "Lead me, O Lord, in Thy righteousness because of mine enemies; make Thy way straight before my face."

With the eager eyes of God, and through the power of His holy Spirit, He can remove obstacles, useless ventures, deception, self deception, and all unseen dangers from the pathways of His earthly creatures. Ps. 121:7-8 tells us, "The Lord shall preserve thy going out and thy coming in from this time forth, and even for evermore." Our God of all grace, purposed, and planned for all human kind (if desired), the way into the light of a spiritual life, that leads us into the knowledge of Him. What would life mean to mankind without God's sheltering love, mercy, and His grace? The Comforter, which is the Holy Ghost sent from above, comforts and cheers us with divine compassion, supplying strength to the utmost parts of our bodies. Step by step, God leads us. We are drawn (John 6:44) by the power of the Holy Spirit into the spiritual path, unto salvation by faith. The Scripture (John 20:31) tells us, "But these are written, that ye might believe that Jesus is the Christ, the Son of God; and that believing ye might have life through His name."

Acknowledging the spiritual walk to gather by faith leads us into the new birth of salvation, which is hidden in our Lord and Savior Jesus Christ. John 3:3 tells us, "Verily, verily, I say unto thee: Except a man be born again, he cannot see the kingdom of God. (Please note vs. 4-7). Again, the new birth is hidden in Jesus Christ, in God the Father. Man was identified (Eph. 1:3-12) in God's purpose and plan of salvation before the foundation of the world. The Scripture (Acts 17:30: tells us, "And the times of this ignorance God winked at, but now commandeth all men every where to repent.

The Scriptures (John 3:16, Luke 23:33, John 19:28-30) tell us that sin was overcome by the power and the sacrifice (Mat. 20:28, Rom. 5:10) of the Father and the Son, noting Calvary.

God's plan of salvation was included in His incessant promises, which were fulfilled (Eph. 1:3-12) in His Son Jesus Christ. "In whom we have redemption through His blood, the forgiveness of sins (v. 1:7), according to the riches of His grace." God made possible the gift of a spiritual life of profound peace, love, and untold joy to all mankind throughout eternity (if desired), nonetheless, man must make the decision.

Tit. 1:2 tells us that In hope of eternal life which God, who cannot lie, promised before the foundation of the world began. The spiritual pathway for mankind was included in God's redemptive plan, regardless of status, rich or poor, race or creed, there is no respect of persons with God. Nonetheless, God's spiritual requirements or demands must be met before mankind can become an heir into His eternal inheritance. 3:7 tells us That being justified by His grace, we should be made heirs according to the hope of eternal life. Tit. 2:11 tells us that For the grace of God that bringeth salvation hath appeared to all men. Every promise of God is sure, the Bible is the Holy word of God. Indeed, God's Word is unchangeable regardless of all individual opinions. Through God's gift of grace, we are blessed with the presence of the Holy Spirit, which is the presence of God in the midst of His children.

The Spirit is made known to the children of God, it flows as on the Day of Pentecost. We must have a clean heart, as the Spirit of God cannot dwell in unclean (I John 4:6, 12-13) temples. "But the fruit of the Spirit is love, joy, peace, long suffering, gentleness, goodness, faith, which cometh by hearing (Gal. 5:22-26) the Word. We have the eternal assurance that we have been delivered from Satan's power, through faith in the blood of our Lord (Eph. 1:11-14), (Col. 1:14-17) and Savior Jesus Christ. After surrendering our lives unto the will of God, we tend to see, feel, and vision the things of life in a different light. We also note, the spiritual harmony of the Spirit of God (Himself) uniting with the inter spirit of mankind. From this true divine influence, one's whole being becomes changed, illuminated by the Spirit of God, noting that the things of the world that once appeared to be very important have indeed lost all attraction. It is a fact that God's redeemed people can vision back with sincere gratitude to God, and look towards the future with eternal hope. Indeed, God is our only hope. He is our fountain of life, He supplies us with enduring strength, lifting us above the snares that we might refrain, overcoming the evils of the world.

Just as miracles were performed through the lives of people centuries ago, that same God is eager to perform miracles in our lives today. We must have steadfast faith (not wavering) in God, and His Word, as nothing is impossible with God. Indeed, nothing can cause God (Is. 42:4) to fail, only trust in Him. It is very true, without faith (Heb. 11:6) man cannot please God. Satan must gloat, understanding the facts of man's language, the doubts, fears and man's deeds. Satan is constantly seeking our thoughts with deceptive (II Cor. 2:11; 11:14) thoughts. Satan was active centuries (Gen. 3:1-9) ago, and he is active today, seeking to bring about discontentment (Rev. 12:9) in the world. "Age is not limited." It is a fact that God's sustaining power is sufficient (Acts 26:18) to persevere, and keep thee in His care.

There have been perilous obstacles in each individual's path of life, some were visible, some were invisible, still, all dangers throughout the universe are visible to God at the same time. It is a noted fact that through the mercy and power of God, many lives have been spared.

The acknowledgment of God's mercy and love, His greatness, and His goodness should not be kept a secret. It should be expounded, made known to all mankind. It is conceivable for one to believe, that there are many individuals who can perceive, visioning back through the scope of time, focusing wholly on God's sustaining mercy, love, and eternal assurance (Acts 16:31).

God's presence is often immediately noted in times of pain, disasters are some critical moments in our lives. It is a fact that man should recognize God's existence, and God's presence at all times, regardless of individual opinions. The Scripture (Prov. 3:6) tells us that In all thy ways acknowledge Him, and He shall direct thy path. God is eager to precede our daily footsteps, and the footsteps of the younger generation. The Scripture (Ps. 91:11) tells us, "For He shall give His angels charge over thee, to keep thee in all thy ways."

Life is living beings, especially human beings, living a course of life in different cultural backgrounds, noting manners and concepts. In our society, the concept of different customs, living conditions, and lifestyles appear as common occurrences. We note and discern ethical values and principles relating to the entity of the human race, as long as the human race exists. Now that knowledge and understanding is contained through wisdom, to depart from the aspects of wisdom, a great risk is imminent, and there are reasonable possibilities of useless ventures (Jas. 3:15-17). It is wise to convey values, the value of knowledge, and the value of understanding, even so, there are possibilities of deception and self-deception. Where there is bitter envying and strife in our hearts, truly, this is not the love of God, nor wisdom from above; this is false wisdom. Prov. 2:6 tells us, "For the Lord givith wisdom: out of His mouth cometh knowledge and understanding. Then shalt thou understand the fear of the Lord, and find the knowledge of God." It is God supplying wisdom into the utmost parts of our capacity of understanding, His counsel givith insight with hope, and assurance at all times. God's Word (Ps. 119:24) is a counselor that advises all mankind. "And this is the confidence that we have in Him, that, if we ask anything according to His will, He heareth us" (I John 5:14-15).

The commandments (Ex. 20:) that were given at Mount Sanai were the Words of God. We note that the Israelites were destroyed because they were disobedient (rebellious) unto God. They were not given the Holy Ghost, but God's holy men were moved by the Holy Ghost (II Pet. 1:21). Now the end of the commandment is charity out of a pure heart, and of a good conscience, and of faith unfeigned (I Tim. 1:5). For all the law is fulfilled in one Word, even in this. "Thou shalt love thy neighbor as thyself." "For the law was given by Moses, but grace and truth came by Jesus Christ." For ye know the grace of our Lord Jesus Christ, that though He was rich, yet for your sakes He became poor, that ye through His poverty might be rich. "For by grace are ye saved through faith; and that not of yourselves: it is the gift of God." God's grace covers all, His mercy and love, redemption, assurance, loving and kindness, peace, and the gift of grace, with much gratefulness for God's eternal favors, noting (I Cor. 10:30). God's love for all mankind is everlasting. The Scripture (Eph. 1:4) tells us that we were chosen in Christ before the foundation of the world.

From Genesis to Revelation the word love is reflected as a warm welcome into the grace of God. Through God's word, we are taught to love one another. Looking back, visioning the narrative of Naomi and Ruth, true love is noted in this story. It is not difficult for one to note the true meaning of love.

It is conceivable for one to believe that the love story of Naomi and Ruth (Ruth 1:-4:) should cause one to pause, take note, and begin to search one's self, recognizing the true meaning of love-the acquired love that God is requesting of all mankind. "Indeed, God is love." Please note; (I John 4:7-11). During the era of the Judges' ruling in Israel, famines were very destructive far and near in the lands, noting the time of Joseph's dwelling in Egypt under Pharaoh's ruling. During the era of the Judges' rule in Israel, the Scripture (Ruth 1-2, 4) tells us that there was a man, and his family living in Bethlehem Judea. The man was Elimelech, his wife was Naomi, who had two sons, because of the famine they settled in Moab. The sons took them wives of Moab. One was Orpha, and the other was Ruth. The sons Mahlon and Chilion died also, and the woman was left of her two sons and her husband. Ruth and her family recognized the sovereignty of God, noting the joyous times of the past that she had enjoyed with her family, now she was alone, with her sister, and her mother-in-law Naomi.

Naomi related insistently to her daughter-in-laws that she deemed it wise that they should go on their way, because she did not have any more sons for them to marry, and she felt she was too old to have a husband. The Scripture (Ruth 1:1-22) tells us they wept. Orpha kissed her mother-in-law Naomi, and went on her way back to her people. Ruth's decision was different from Orpha's decision. Ruth was determined to look after her mother-in-law Naomi, noting the fact that she was all alone. Ruth was concerned and she was devoted to her mother-in-law.

Ruth was so devoted to Naomi that she made a vow revealing her loyalty and her faithfulness, making them inseparable. The Scripture (Ruth 1:16-19) tells us, "And Ruth said, Entreat me not to leave thee, or to return from following after thee: for whither thou goest-I will go; and where thou lodgest, I will lodge: thy people shall be my people, and thy God my God.

It is conceivable for one to believe that Ruth trusted in the God of Abraham, Isaac, and Jacob, the God of Israel. Naomi and Ruth returned to Bethlehem. Indeed, they were not alone, because God was with them, to bless, lead, and guide them.

Remember the former things of old. I am God, and there is none like Me. Indeed, Ruth will be divinely rewarded for her kind and loving deeds. Rom. 13:10 tells us that Love worketh no ill to his neighbor, therefore, love is the fulfilling of the law. "God is love."

It is conceivable to believe that Ruth, the Moabitess, was making known to the whole world the true concern of her heart, which was the welfare of her mother-in-law Naomi. God is wholly able to give and fill the hearts of all mankind with true love. God is also eager to remove the stony hearts from all mankind, and fill each heart with divine love from above (Ezek. 11:19-20). Rom. 13:8 tells us, "Owe no man any thing, but to love one another: for he that loveth another hath fulfilled the law."

Returning to Bethlehem, Ruth had to provide for her mother-in-law. Ruth decided to glean in the fields, picking up what was left behind the reapers, which had fallen upon the ground. Ruth was contented, gleaming in the barley fields at a distance behind the reapers, she was aware that ample food for both she and her mother-in-law Naomi would be supplied.

It is a fact that God was with Ruth, leading and guiding her footsteps towards great rewards, which she very much deserved. "...If God be for us, who can be against us....?

From day to day, Ruth gleaned in the fields during the barley harvest. It is conceivable to believe that Ruth was not always aware of whose field she entered to glean daily, but God was aware of her daily footsteps; besides, Ruth the Moabitess left her father and mother to follow her mother-in-law Naomi to a land where she knew not the people in Bethlehem. Nonetheless, Ruth was eager to glean in the corn and wheat fields, that she and Naomi might have food to eat.

Ruth went on her way to glean in the field after the reapers. She was not aware of the fact that she was gleaning in the field of Boaz, who was a wealthy Bethlemite (2:1, 8-18). Boaz was a bachelor, a mighty man of wealth. Boaz saw Ruth then he questioned his servant (2, 3, 5), "Whose damsel is this?" The servant related to Boaz that Ruth was the Moabitish damsel that returned with Naomi out of the country of Moab.

It is very possible Boaz saw much more than beauty when he observed Ruth. Boaz also saw the marks of character and beauty, a drawing attraction that impressed him so much he sought to keep Ruth gleaning in his field. Boaz made known his favor to Ruth. He instructed her to abide by his maidens, he also made very certain that Ruth felt safe and wanted. "He comforted her." The Lord recompense thy work, and a full reward be given thee of the Lord God of Israel, under whose wings thou art come to trust. Ruth worshiped and trusted in the God of Israel, who was the God of patriarch Abraham, Isaac, and Jacob.

Boaz sought the proper means that he might purposely redeem the inheritance, making possible his marriage to Ruth. Boaz followed the demanded rules and redeemed the inheritance (4:).

Ruth became Boaz's wife. They had a son, his name was Obed. He was the father of Jesse, the father of David. The Scripture (I Chr. 11:47) tells us that Obed was one of David's mighty men. It was through Ruth's marriage to Boaz that she became an ancestor of Christ. "...If God be for us, who can be against us....? And though I have the gift of prophecy, and understand all mysteries and all knowledge, and though I have all faith, so that I could remove mountains, and have not charity, I am nothing. And though I bestow all my goods to feed the poor, and though I give my body to be burned, and have not charity, it profiteth me nothing: Charity suffereth long, and is kind; charity envieth not; charity vaunteth not itself, is not puffed up. Doth not behave itself unseemly, seeketh not her own, is not easily provoked, thinketh no evil. Rejoiceth not in iniquity, but rejoiceth in truth; Beareth all things, believeth all things, hopeth all things, endureth all things. Charity never faileth: but whether there be prophecies, they shall fail; whether there be tongues, they shall cease; whether there be knowledge, it shall vanish away (I Cor. 13:2-8, 13)." And now abideth faith, hope, charity, these three; but the greatest of these is charity. He that loveth not knoweth not God; for God is love. "For God so loved the world, that He gave His only begotten Son, that whosoever believeth in Him should not perish, but have everlasting life."

> "Thou art worthy, O Lord,
> to receive glory and honor and power:
> for Thou hast created all things,
> and for Thy pleasure they are and were created."

chapter 8

Facts and Subjective Ideas

Foundation and Preparation for Youth Success

Webster's Dictionary defines youth as the quality or stage of being young, youthness, juvenility: The part of life coming between childhood, and maturity, adolescence; also an early stage of youth or existence, possessing youth, not yet old or mature. Youth is also a stage lately begun, not advanced or developed, still in early stages (teenagers), lacking experience, immature. In fact, the eyes are noted as having the bright clear keenness associated with youth, hopeful, and cheerful. Throughout the past or passing years of youthful development, periodically, many changes are noted (age is not limited). It is then that many truths become reality, part of one's being.

In the path of life, the time or moment is sure to come when each individual must go his/her way in life, and seek the factual realities of adult living. There are many helpful qualities such as being responsible, reliable, and self-assured. One must be prepared to obtain independent living. In due time those youthful footsteps are sure to become unforgettable memories, noting back to yester-years. It is wise to prepare early in life for future goals. It is also good judgment, and very important (crucial) to ponder the desired goals with future vision. One must be prepared to meet the challenges of independent living, i.e., adulthood, the state of being adult.

It is very essential to note that a good foundation can or will become an asset towards one's future goals, noting classroom attention, stabilization, attitude, self-control, self-esteem, and motivation. These individual qualities can only lead to future goals with excellent success, noting charity.

It is also important to note that those youthful years should be an achieving time, with steadfast faith in one's self, aware of the fact that one can become the person that one is desiring to be. One's determination holds the key to success.

Webster's Dictionary defines study as fixing the mind closely upon a subject; The applying of the mind attentively, to acquire knowledge; To dwell upon something in thought, to ponder. The acquired qualities are preparations that leads as a guide to a life of future success. Sports are also noted. "Why should one chose to live a deploring life?" There are many paths in life, some are true, real, and some are false. Ponder the path of thy feet, and let all thy ways be established. Lest thou shouldest ponder the path of life, her ways are movable, that thou canst not know them (Prov. 4:26, 5:6).

Life is indeed a precious gift. The gift of life comes from God, the Creator, ruler and maker of all that exists. God is in the foreknowledge (Eph. 1:3-4) of all things.

It is conceivable to note that sometimes it is very wise to divert, change, or turn aside from a course of life; and go in the way of knowledge and understanding, visioning through the scope of time, in hope of a brighter and promotive course in life. Seeking vocational guidance is very important.

The gift of wisdom is given to man. Who giveth wisdom? For the Lord giveth wisdom, out of His mouth (Prov. 2:6) cometh knowledge and understanding. It is God supplying wisdom into the utmost parts of our minds. Indeed, His counsel imparts enhancing insight and assurance. Now that knowledge and understanding are contained through wisdom, to depart from the aspects of wisdom a great risk is imminent, there are reasonable possibilities of useless ventures. There is true wisdom from above, first pure, peaceful, and gentle. Where there is bitter envying and strife within our hearts, this is not wisdom from above, this is false wisdom, without knowledge or good judgment.

It is wise to convey values, the value of knowledge, and the value of understanding. Even so, there are possibilities of deception and self-deception. "Too many aspects are viewed from an outward appearance or pleasing assertions: It is wise to note: Views and assertions are sometimes over-shadowed with hidden deception, and eventually is proven to be false or fatal." It is not impossible for one to be deceived. "Only God is a discerner of the thoughts and intents of the heart." (Heb. 4:12). It is the wisdom of the Spirit, which is God uniting with the human spirit of mankind, safeguarding and controlling man's going out, and man's coming. It is the indwelling Spirit of God that restores one's health and strength (Is. 53:5), which is the controlling influence of the Spirit of God, noting the renewing (Rom. 12:2) of the mind. "Indeed, God is the author of knowledge and understanding, His wisdom is unsearchable." We note that the flesh is prone to weaken (Mat. 26:41) because of spiritual instability. The Scripture (I Cor. 11:28) says, "...But let a man examine himself...."

Life is very precious, each individual has a life to live, none other can live it, nevertheless, in the twinkle of an eye, fate can destroy it. Life is like a mist, we have it, and it vanishes away. It is always wise to ponder and observe the path of thy feet. "But the end of all things is at hand (1 Pet. 4:7): be ye therefore sober, and watch unto prayer." Obedience is noted.

Again, life is very precious. Life's values and principles are noted to be followed for a lifetime. Be strong, watchful, and steadfast, having total faith in your given abilities, noting the fact that there are activating forces in the world as that of gravity, seeking to debase or destroy one's future goals. It is always wise to seek parental guidance and vocational guidance. This will prove to be an asset towards your future goals.

Opportunities are available now awaiting the seekers. One must not be, nor remain, willfully blind. Success is available. Now is the time to achieve, age is not limited. If dropped out of school, find quiet time to ponder with vision, try to discern what is progressive, and what is useless ventures. Knowledge is the key that will open doors that once were closed. Try to retrace the footsteps of the past, find your way back into some educational facility, seeking vocational guidance. It is not wise to act and think later. Why should one choose to live a deploring life? Now is the right time to seek and accomplish the desired goals, as man cannot turn back the hands of time.

From time to time, visible changes arise and develop. It is then many truths are noted. Those memorable years of youth will come to an end, again, one must be prepared to meet the challenges of independent living, i.e., adulthood. It is very important to note the fact that parents are still there for you, to offer guidance and support towards your future goals. It is also wise to find quiet time, and seek divine guidance. "From within, a soft voice will enter the mind:" And thine ears shall hear a word behind thee, saying: This is the way, walk ye in it, when ye turn to the right hand, and when ye turn to the left (Is. 30:21). "Every word of God is pure: He is a shield (Prov. 30:5) unto them that put their trust in Him."

In the path of life, it is possible and quite simple to form the inception of habits and patterns, unaware of the future effects upon one's life, only time will be a noted factor. Eventually, it is noted, one's life gradually change developing into pronounced patterns, causing individuals to ponder or question one's actions or behavior.

It is noted that some habits and patterns are valid, healthy, and productive while there are others that are self-deceptive, appearing to degenerate one's life, noting the mind.

It is wise to stop and ponder, noting how we employ, or how we are going to employ our lives. "Lest thou ponder the path of life, her ways are movable (unstable) that thou canst not know them" (Prov. 5:6). Habits and patterns are the ways of an acquired lifestyle, usually easy to acquire, but the acquired effects can prove to remain an indefinite time. The abstraction of abstaining power, controlling one's self is noted (impaired); seemingly ideas are perceived in a different light. The manner of insolence, divisiveness, and the refusal of guidance is noted. It is a fact that some habits and patterns are questionable.

Good health habits can only mean a healthy life, which is a constant human desire. Good health habits and patterns should be one of life's first priorities or expectations. It is conceivable to note that self-reliance appears to be a noted factor; self-distrust is a possibility, noting obedience.

God is the author of knowledge and understanding, and His wisdom is unsearchable.

It is impossible to be misled by the Word of God, His counsel is mine, and sound wisdom; I am understanding; I have strength. Through the grace of God, I have hope. The gift of wisdom is given to man, which is a gift (Ex. 31:3) from God. It is God supplying wisdom, (by His Spirit) into the utmost realm of the minds of mankind. Mat. 7:7 tells us, "Ask, and it shall be given you; seek, and you shall find; knock, and it shall be open unto you."

It is very important to note, recognizing the unlimited power and perfection of God that everything God made was good. Man can observe and feel the touch of God's power, noting the air that we breathe, it cannot be seen, nonetheless, we are aware that it does exist, because we are alive.

"For the invisible things of Him from the creation of the world are clearly seen, being understood by the things that are made, even His eternal power and God-head; so that they are without excuse" (Rom. 1:20).

God's existence and God's presence was observed by our first parents, in the garden of Eden. God's existence is noted today, and will be noted throughout eternity.

From season to season nature appears in many different forms, all under and in obedience to the will of God. We observe mother nature in form, and natural scenery of flowering beauty the year around; colorful blossoms with fragrances that were not made by mankind. Each blossom both large and small, appears to be relating a message, solemnly whispering a speechless living testimony: "There is a Great God with all authority, and perfection; who is all knowledge (wisdom) and understanding; God is aware of all the mysteries" (Acts 2:23; Deut. 29:29).

Again, God's existence, and God's presence can be observed throughout the universe if spiritually discerned. In the moveless sky man can sometimes observe the visible heavenly bodies, all functioning within their given divine courses, noting the Solar System with timed revolving heavenly bodies.

We see the sun, moon, and shooting stars (Jer. 51:15), all functioning divinely in their given courses. The sun and moon sending out light and warmth throughout the world, under the power and command of God. One can observe the forceful billows rolling upon the flowing waters. The timely tides can be seen forcefully dashing upon the shores, coming in and going out at the appointed time. We see and feel the falling rain drops as they fall upon the thirsty lands far and near. We see the lightning flashing and we hear the thunder discharging the noise of a blast, activated by the power of God.

Beautiful is the azure sky, with its unfading color that all mankind can admire, giving God all the praise and glory.

It is noted, all of God's earthly creatures respond in obedience according to truth, regularity, kind, sort, character, species, affection, and naturalness, noting the creation. It does appear that God's earthly creatures have acquired an inborn tendency to behave in a way characteristic of species. They are noted going out, and returning to their own habitation. It is a fact that God provides for all of His creatures. "Behold the fowls of the air: for they sow not, neither do they reap, nor gather into barns; yet your heavenly Father feedeth them." Are ye not much better than they? Man was created (Gen. 1:26-27) in the image of God (noting Gen. 2:7). Man was created for God's pleasure and glory (Is. 43:7; Rev. 4:11). "God is the Creator of a great creation" (Please note Ps. 104:30-31).

These are all divine creations with divine authority and perfection without modification. It is a fact that only God could have placed them within their given places.

I have declared the former things from the beginning, and they went forth out of my mouth, and I showed them; I did them suddenly, and they came to pass. They are created now, and not from the beginning, even before the day when thou heardest them not; lest thou say: Behold, I knew them (Is. 48:3, 7). "Remember the former things of old: for I am God, and there is none else; I am God, and there is none like Me (46:9)." Mine hand also hath laid the foundation of the earth, and my right hand hath spanned the heavens. When I call unto them, they stand up together (48:13). "Look unto Me, and be ye saved, all the ends of the earth: for I am God, and there is none else (45:22). Remember now thy Creator in the days of thy youth, while the evil days come not, nor the years draw nigh, when thou shalt say, I have no pleasure in them."

Again, obedience also leads to success and should be acquired early in one's life. "Train up a child the way he should go: (Prov. 22:6) and when he is old, he will not depart from it." It is noted that good self-control, foundation and preparation brings into focus good lifetime habits and patterns. Col. 3:20 tells us, "Children obey your parents in all things: for this is well pleasing unto the Lord." Obedience is the act or habit of obeying, noting submission to authority. Prov. 9:11 tells us "For by Me thy days shall be multiplied, and the years of thy life shall be increased." Obedience is very necessary.

Again, God was/is concerned about the souls of all mankind. Before the world began, man was identified (Eph. 1:4) chosen in Christ (Col. 1:14-15), before the foundation of the World. "For the Lord of hosts hath purposed, and who shall disannul it? and His hand is stretched out, who shall turn it back?" God was in the foreknowledge of man's sinful nature, and the sinful state (Gen. 3:1-3, 6-13) of all mankind (Rom. 5:12). Salvation was planned (Eph. 1:3-12) in eternity, noting (John 3:16). The Scripture (Rom. 3:23) tells us, "For all have sinned, and come short of the glory of God," noting (v. 24). "Now faith is the substance of things hoped for, the evidence of things not seen." "But let him ask in faith-nothing wavering...." Put on the whole armor of God, that ye may be able to stand against the wiles of the devil (Eph. 6:11-18). The Scripture (James 3:) unfolds the evil manner and the dangerous habits of the tongue. "For every kind of beasts, and of birds, and of serpents, and of things in the sea, is tamed, and hath been tamed of mankind: But the tongue can no man tame; it is an unruly evil, full of deadly poison." Wisdom is the principle thing; therefore get wisdom. And with all thy getting get understanding. (Prov. 3:7). Submit yourselves therefore to God. Resist the devil, and he will flee from you. (Jas. 4:7). But the God of all grace, who hath called us unto His eternal glory by Christ Jesus, after that ye have suffered awhile, make you perfect, stablish, strengthen, settle you (I Pet. 5:10). "I am the vine, ye are the branches: He that abideth in Me, and I in him, the same bringeth forth much fruit: for without Me ye can do nothing." (John 15:5).

"For I am persuaded, that neither death, nor life, nor angels, nor principalities, nor powers, nor things present, nor things to come: Nor height, nor depth, nor any other creature, shall be able to separate us from the love of God, which is in Christ Jesus our Lord (Rom. 8:38-39)."

> Thou art worthy, O Lord,
> to receive glory and honor and power:
> for Thou hast created all things,
> and for Thy pleasure they are and were created (Rev. 4:11)

chapter 9

Scriptures for Divine Guidance

According to His divine power he hath given unto us all things that pertain unto life and godliness, through the knowledge of Him that hath called us to glory and virtue. Whereby are given unto us exceeding great and precious promises: that by these ye might be partakers of the divine nature, having escaped the corruption that is in the world through lust. And beside this, giving all diligence, add to your faith virtue; and to virtue knowledge: And to knowledge temperance; and to temperance patience; and to patience godliness: And to godliness brotherly kindness; and to brotherly kindness; charity. For if these things be in you, and abound, they make you that ye shall neither be barren nor unfruitful in the knowledge of our Lord Jesus Christ. But he that lacketh these things is blind, and cannot see afar off, and hath forgotten that he was purged from his old sins (II Pet. 1:3-9).

For if God spared not the angles that sinned, but cast them down to hell, and delivered them into chains of darkness, to be reserved unto judgment. And spared not the old world, but saved Noah the eighth person, a preacher of righteousness, bringing in the flood upon the world, of the ungodly (II Pet. 2:4-5; 21).

I will instruct thee and teach in the way which thou shalt go: I will guide thee with mine eye (Ps. 32:8).

Rejoice in the Lord, O ye righteous: for praise is comely for the upright. Praise the Lord with harp: sing unto Him with the psaltery and an instrument of ten strings. Sing unto Him a new song; play skillfully with a loud noise. For the word of the Lord is right; and all His works are done in truth. He loveth righteousness and judgment: the earth is full of the goodness of the Lord. By the word of the Lord were the heavens made; and all the host of them by the breath of His mouth. For He spake, and it was done; He commanded, and it stood fast. The Lord bringeth the counsel of the heathen to nought: He maketh the devices of the people of none effect. The counsel of the Lord standeth forever, the thoughts of His heart to all generations (Ps. 33:1-6, 9-12).

The steps of a good man are ordered by the Lord: and he delighteth in his way. Though he fall, he shall not be utterly cast down: for the Lord upholdeth him with His right hand. I have been young, and now am old; yet have I not seen the righteous forsaken, nor his seed begging bread (Ps. 37:23-25).

The Lord is my shepherd; I shall not want. He maketh me to lie down in green pastures: He leadeth me beside the still waters. He restoreth my soul: He leadeth me in the paths of righteousness for His name's sake. Yea, though I walk through the valley of the shadow of death, I will fear no evil: for thou art with me; thy rod and thy staff they comfort me. Thou preparest a table before me in the presence of mine enemies: thou anointest my head with oil; my cup runneth over. Surely goodness and mercy shall follow me all the days of my life: and I will dwell in the house of the Lord for ever (Ps. 23:1-6).

Unto thee, O Lord, do I lift up my soul. O my God, I trust in thee: let me not be ashamed, let not mine enemies triumph over me. Yea, let none that wait on thee be ashamed which transgress without cause. Show me thy ways, O Lord; teach me thy paths. Lead me in thy truth, and teach me: for thy art the God of my salvation; on thee do I wait all the day. Remember, O Lord, thy tender mercies and thy loving kindnesses; for they have been ever of old. Remember not the sins of my youth, nor my transgressions: according to thy mercy remember thou me for thy goodness' sake, O Lord. Good and upright is the Lord: therefore will He teach sinners in the way. The meek will He guide in judgment: and the meek will he teach His way (Ps. 25:1-9).

I will say of the Lord, He is my refuge and my fortress: My God; in Him will I trust. Surely He shall deliver thee from the snare of the fowler, and from the noisome pestilence. He shall cover thee with his feathers, and under his wings shall thou trust: His truth shall be thy shield and buckler. Thou shalt not be afraid for the terror by night; nor for the arrow that flieth by day; nor for the pestilence that walketh in darkness; nor for the destruction that wasteth at noonday. A thousand shall fall at thy side, and ten thousand at thy right hand; but it shall not come nigh thee. Only with thine eyes shalt thou behold and see the reward of the wicked. Because thou hast made the Lord, which is my refuge, even the Most High, thy habitation; there shall no evil befall thee, neither shall any plague come nigh thy dwelling. For He shall give His angels charge over thee, to keep thee in all thy ways (Ps. 91:2-11).

Give instruction to a wise man, and he will be yet wiser: teach a just man, and he will increase in learning. The fear of the Lord is the beginning of wisdom: and the knowledge of the Holy is understanding. For by Me thy days shall be multiplied, and the years of thy life shall be increased. If thou be wise, thou shalt be wise for thyself: but if thou scornest, thou alone shalt bear it (Prov. 9:9-12).

But we are all as an unclean thing, and all our righteousness are as filthy rags; and we all do fade as a leaf; and our iniquities, like the wind, have taken us away. And there is none that calleth upon thy name, that stirreth up himself to take hold of thee: for thou hast hid thy face from us, and hast consumed us, because of our iniquities. But now, O Lord, thou art our father; we are the clay, and thou our potter; and we are all the work of thy hand (Is. 64:6-8).

Who hath measured the waters in the hollow of His hand, and meted out heaven with the span, and comprehended the dust of the earth in a measure, and weighed the mountains in scales, and the hills in a balance? Who hath directed the spirit of the Lord, or being His counsel or hath tought him? Have ye not known? have ye not heard? hath it not been told you from the beginning? have ye not understood from the foundation of the earth? It is He that sitteth upon the circle of the earth, and the inhabitants thereof are as grasshoppers; that stretcheth out the heavens as a curtain, and spreadeth them out as a tent to dwell in: To whom then will ye liken Me, or shall I be equal? saith the Holy One. Lift up your eyes on high, and behold who hath created these things, that bringeth out their host by number: He calleth them all by names by the greatness of His might, for that He is strong in power; not one faileth. Why sayeth thou, O Jacob, and speakest O Israel: My way is hid from the Lord, and my judgment is passed over from my God? Hast thou not known? hast thou not heard, that the everlasting God, the Lord, the Creator of the ends of the earth, fainteth not, neither is weary? There is no searching of His understanding (Is. 40:12-13; 21-22; 25-28).

For the Lord thy God is a merciful God; He will not forsake thee, neither destroy thee, nor forget the covenant of thy fathers which He sware unto them. Know therefore this day, and consider it in thine heart, that the Lord He is God in heaven above, and upon the earth beneath: there is none else. Thou shalt keep therefore His statutes, and His commandments, which I command thee this day, that it may go well with thee, and with thy children after thee, and that thou mayest prolong thy days upon the earth, which the Lord thy God giveth thee, forever (Deut. 4:31, 39-40).

Finally, my brethren, be strong in the Lord, and in the power of His might. Put on the whole armor of God, that ye may be able to stand against the wiles of the devil. For we wrestle not against flesh and blood, but against principalities, against powers, against the rulers of the darkness of this world, against spiritual wickedness in high places. Wherefore take unto you the whole armor of God, that ye may be able to with-stand in the evil day, and having done all, to stand. (Eph. 6:10-13).

Is any among you afflicted? let him pray. Is any merry? let him sing psalms. Is any sick among you? let him call for the elders of the church; and let them pray over him, anointing him with oil in the name of the Lord: And the prayer of faith shall save the sick, and the Lord shall raise him up; and if he have committed sins, they shall be forgiven him. Confess your faults one to another, and pray one for another, that ye may be healed. The effectual fervent prayer of a righteous man availeth much. Eli'jah was a man subject to like passions as we are, and he prayed earnestly that it might not rain: and it rained not on the earth by the space of three years and six months. And he prayed again, and the heaven gave rain, and the earth brought forth her fruit (Jas. 5:13-18).

Now faith is the substance of things hoped for, the evidence of things not seen. For by it the elders obtained a good report. Through faith we understand that the worlds were framed by the Word of God, so that things which are seen were not made of things which do appear. By faith Abel offered unto God a more excellent sacrifice than Cain, by which he obtained witness that he was righteous, God testifying of his gift: and by it he being dead yet speaketh. By faith Abraham, when he was tried, offered up Isaac: and he that had received the promises offered up his only begotten son: Of whom it was said, That in Isaac shall thy seed be called (Heb. 11:1-4, 17-18). Looking unto Jesus the author and finisher of our faith; who for the joy that was set before Him endured the cross, despising the shame, and set down at the right hand of the throne of God (12:2).

Brethren, if a man be overtaken in a fault, ye which are spiritual, restore such a one in the spirit of meekness; considering thyself, lest thou also be tempted. Bear ye one another's burdens, and so fulfill the law of Christ. For if a man think himself to be something, when he is nothing, he deceiveth himself. But let every man prove himself his own work, and then shall he have rejoicing in himself alone, and not in another. For every man shall bear his own burden. Let him that is tought in the word communicate unto him that teacheth in all good things. "Be not deceived; God is not mocked: for whatsoever a man soweth, that shall he also reap" (Gal. 6:1-7).

Even so the tongue is a little member, and boasteth great things. Behold, how great a matter a little fire kindleth! And the tongue is a fire, a world of iniquity: so is the tongue among our members, that it defileth the whole body, and setteth on fire the course of nature; and it is set on fire of hell. For every kind of beasts, and of birds, and of serpents, and of things in the sea, is tamed, and hath been tamed of mankind: But the tongue can no man tame; it is an unruly evil, full of deadly poison. Who is a wise man and endued with knowledge among you? Let him show out of a good conversation his works with meekness of wisdom. But if ye have bitter envying and strife in your hearts, glory not, and lie not against the truth. This wisdom descendeth not from above, but is earthly, sensual, devilish. For where envying and strife is, there is confusion and every evil work (Jas. 3:5-8; 13-16).

In the fear of the Lord is strong confidence: and His children shall have a place of refuge. The fear of the Lord is the fountain of life, to depart from the snares of death. Wisdom resteth in the heart of him that hath understanding: but that which is in the midst of fools is made known. Righteousness exalteth a nation: but sin is a reproach to any people. The king's favor is towards a wise servant: but his wrath is against him that causeth shame (Prov. 14:26-27, 33-35). I will make waste mountains and hills, and dry up all their herbs; and I will make the rivers islands, and I will dry up the pools. And I will bring the blind by a way that they know not; I will lead them in paths that they have not known: I will make darkness light before them, and crooked things straight. These things will I do unto them, and not forsake them (Is. 42:15-16).

A thousand shall fall at thy side, and ten thousand at thy right hand, but it shall not come nigh thee. Only with thine eyes shalt thou behold and see the reward of the wicked. Because thou hast made the Lord, which is my refuge, even the Most High, thy habitation; there shall no evil befall thee, neither shall any plague come nigh thy dwelling. For He shall give His angels charge over thee, to keep thee in all thy ways. They shall bear thee up in their hands, lest thou dash thy foot against a stone. Thou shalt tread upon the lion and adder: the young lion and the dragon shalt thou trample under feet. Because He hath set his love upon me, therefore will I deliver him: I will set him on high, because he hath known my name. He shall call upon Me, and I will answer him: I will be with him in trouble; I will deliver him, and honor him. With long life will I satisfy him, and show him My salvation (Ps. 91:7-16).

Behold the Lord God will come with strong hand, and His arm shall rule for Him: behold, His reward is with Him, and His work before Him. He shall feed His flock like a shepherd: He shall gather the lambs with His arm, and carry them in His bosom, and shall gently lead those that are with young. Who hath measured the waters in the hollow of His hand, and meted out heaven with the span, and comprehended the dust of the earth in a measure, and weighed the mountains in scales, and the hills in a balance. Who hath directed the spirit of the Lord? or being His counselor hath tought Him? With whom took he counsel, and who instructed Him, and tought Him in the path of judgment, and tought Him knowledge, and showed to Him the way of understanding? To whom then will ye liken God? or what likeness will ye compare unto Him? Have ye not known? have ye not heard? hath it not been told you from the beginning? have ye not understood from the foundation of the earth? It is He that sitteth upon the circle of the earth, and the inhabitants thereof are as grasshoppers; that stretcheth out the heavens as a curtain, and spreadeth them out as a tent to dwell in. Hast thou not known? hast thou not heard, that the everlasting God, their Lord, the Creator of the ends of the earth, fainteth not, neither is weary? There is no searching of His understanding. He giveth power to the faint; and to them that have no might He increaseth strength. Even the youths shall faint and be weary, and the young men shall utterly fall; But they that wait upon the Lord shall renew their strength; they shall mount up with wings as eagles; they shall run, and not be weary; and they shall walk, and not faint (Is. 40:10-14, 18, 21-22, 28-31).

Children, obey your parents in the Lord: for this is right. Honor thy father and mother; which is the first commandment with promise: That it may be well with thee, and thou mayest live long on the earth. And ye fathers provoke not your children to wrath: but bring them up in the nurture and admonition of the Lord (Eph. 6:1-4).

In the beginning God created the heaven and the earth (Gen. 1:1).

In the beginning was the Word, and the Word was with God, and Word was God. The same was in the beginning with God. All things were made by Him; and without Him was not any thing made that was made. In Him was life; and the life was the light of men (John 1:1-4).

Remember the former things of old: for I am God and there is none else; I am God, and there is none like Me. Declaring the end from the beginning, and from ancient times the things that are not yet done, saying, My counsel shall stand, and I will do all my pleasure (Is. 46:9-10).

According as He hath chosen us in Him before the foundation of the world, that we should be holy and without blame before Him in love (Eph. 1:4).

Wherefore, as by one man sin entered into the world and death by sin; and so death passed upon all men, for that all have sinned: For all have sinned, and come short of the glory of God; Being justified freely by His grace through the redemption that is in Christ Jesus: Whom God hath set forth to be a propitiation through faith in His blood, to declare His righteousness for the remission of sins that are past, through the forbearance of God (Rom. 5:12; 3:23-25).

Even when we were dead in sins hath quickened us together with Christ, (by grace ye are saved); For by grace are ye saved through faith; and that not of yourselves: it is the gift of God (Eph. 2:5; 8).

Not by works of righteousness which we have done, but according to His mercy He saved us, by the washing of regeneration, and renewing of the Holy Ghost; Which He shed on us abundantly through Jesus Christ our Savior; That being justified by His grace, we should be made heirs according to the hope of eternal life (Tit. 3:5-7).

For the preaching of the cross is to them that perish foolishness; but unto us which are saved it is the power of God (I Cor. 1:18).

"For whosoever shall call upon the name of the Lord shall be saved (Rom. 10:13).

For God so loved the world, that He gave His only begotten Son, that whosoever believeth in Him should not perish, but have everlasting life" (John 3:16).